12-05-2007

For Anthony and Amanda
I hope it will give you
blissful experiences
Thanks for heaving me in you're home.

TANTRA

T
THE
A
ART OF
N
MIND-BLOWING
T
SEX
R
VAL SAMPSON
A

LONDON

DEDICATION

This book is dedicated to my husband Colin, with my heartfelt gratitude for his enduring love and support, and to my son, Oliver, whose presence fills me with hope, comfort and joy.

ACKNOWLEDGEMENTS

I would like to thank all the friends and Tantra teachers who have given me invaluable help with this book, especially Dagmar Charlton; Leora Lightwoman; Karen Goodwin; Gweneth Roberts; Dominic Fielder; Peter Barker; Ros Barker; John Hawken and David Secombe.

3 5 7 9 10 8 6 4 2

First published in 2002
This edition published in 2004 by Vermilion, an imprint of Ebury Press, Random House, 20 Vauxhall Bridge Road, London SW1V 2SA

www.randomhouse.co.uk

Random House Australia (Pty) Limited, 20 Alfred Street, Milsons Point, Sydney, New South Wales 2061, Australia

Random House New Zealand Limited, 18 Poland Road, Glenfield, Auckland 10, New Zealand

Random House South Africa (Pty) Limited, Endulini, 5A Jubilee Road, Parktown 2193, South Africa

The Random House Group Limited Reg. No. 954009

Papers used by Vermilion are natural, recyclable products made from wood grown in sustainable forests.

Printed and bound in Singapore by Tien Wah Press

A CIP catalogue record for this book is available from the British Library

ISBN 0 09 189476 X
ISBN 9780091894764 (from January 2007)

contents

This book began life as an idea for a short article. As a journalist, I've covered everything from complementary medicine to celebrity interviews, but when I suggested a piece on Tantra to a national newspaper, I had no idea of what really lay ahead. I thought it sounded like a sexy, fun subject that would spice up dinner-party conversations and impress my friends, so to be honest, it was rather a shallow impulse that sparked my interest. But the more I read about Tantra the more fascinated I became. I ended up spending a year researching the subject and interviewing dozens of people. It would turn out to be one of the most interesting projects of my career, and one that would have a profound effect on me.

Tantra is a 5000-year-old spiritual tradition, but its relevance to 21st century society is astonishing. It offers an approach that enables women to feel sexually confident and good about themselves, and gives men an opportunity to become multi-orgasmic and to satisfy their lovers in the most intimate, soulful ways. It gives new lovers a unique way of getting to know each other on a deep and connected level, and also enables couples who have been together for years to find the passion they may have thought they'd lost.

It was watching a couple regain this level of intimacy on the first Tantra workshop I ever attended that made me want to write this book. I had turned up at a venue in north London one Friday night, intending to observe the workshop, safely hidden behind my notebook. My attitude was that everyone was probably slightly sex-mad, but the experience would be harmless and a bit of a laugh. I had practically made up my mind that if I thought Tantra was a waste of time I could write a light-hearted piece, poking gentle fun at it.

Then, on the first evening, one man sat in our circle and said that the only reason he was there was because his wife had dragged him along, and he hinted that he'd only turn up the next day if he couldn't think of a good enough reason to get out of it. I felt some sympathy for him.

But by the Sunday afternoon, the end of the course, he had been transformed. After 28 years of marriage he turned to his wife with adoration in his eyes and declared how deeply he loved her. And I found that my mind had been changed, too. Anything that could restore that level of passion in a relationship that was 28 years old deserved serious consideration.

Afterwards I stayed in touch with the couple to see if the husband's emotions that day had simply been down to a burst of over-enthusiasm after a fun weekend. They had not. Both partners have continued their interest in Tantra and both believe it has put them in touch with levels of love and understanding they had never before experienced.

At first, I thought Tantra would be the kind of subject that I could simply interview other people about. But I soon realised that Tantra is a practical tool. You have to experience it in order for it to make real sense. So I have continued participating in workshops and made efforts to incorporate Tantric practices in my own life.

Tantra has revolutionised my ideas about sex and relationships. Not only does it offer a blueprint for great sex with another person, it gives each individual the chance to experience their own sexual energy and to use it creatively in every aspect of their life. It is a mind-blowing discovery.

Changing your attitude to sex takes time. It is not compulsory to drop everything that you have enjoyed or found fun before – in fact, it's vital that you don't. But you do have to be prepared to widen your horizons and accept that there is more to sex than the occasional mindless bonk that most people settle for at some stage in their lives. If you have an open mind, then this is the book for you.

Changing your attitude to sex takes time. It is not compulsory to drop everything that you have enjoyed or found fun before

Introduction: What is Tantra?

Ask a roomful of couples with children, jobs and mortgages to raise their hands if their sex lives are blissful and you'll probably get no raised hands, a few hoots of laughter and plenty of embarrassed shoulder-shrugging. After all, everyone's love life gets submerged by stress at work, hassle at home and sheer exhaustion, doesn't it? Isn't sex meant to start out exciting and end up cosy, if you are one of the lucky few, or almost non-existent, if you are one of the majority?

It is received wisdom in the West that sexual relationships peak with the excitement of newness at the beginning and then dwindle downhill. But it doesn't have to be this way. There is a direct route to rekindling sexuality and bringing depth and richness to your relationship. It is a kind of sex education for grown-ups. It's called Tantra.

Tantra is a philosophy that offers an entirely natural way of achieving blissful experiences. It doesn't require any artificial stimulants. As a society we have lost touch with our natural abilities to transcend our routine existence, as can be seen from the widespread incidence of drug abuse. A report in *The Times* in March 2001, for example, describes the appeal of crack cocaine: '[It gives] that giddying collapse into sensual ecstasy … [for] thirty minutes of bliss before you are craving it again.' Tantra offers a superior, longer, and entirely natural high.

The popular misconception is that Tantric sex is ordinary sex that goes on for hours and hours. The truth is, however, that it offers an entirely different approach. In the first place, it is not confined to the genitals; orgasms can be experienced throughout the whole body. And by learning some simple physical processes, you can powerfully enrich your emotional and spiritual life.

We all have a life-enhancing and cleansing energy stored in our bodies. Meditation, yoga and some types of rhythmic dancing all offer ways of accessing this energy. But Tantric sex not only helps you to get in touch with this energy, it teaches you to use it for your emotional and spiritual wellbeing. Instead of sex being a purely physical experience – a kind of genital sneeze – it becomes a way of opening your heart and mind to the purest forms of love and unity. You become inspired by greater levels of passion and pleasure than you may have thought possible.

LINDA, 34, MARKETING MANAGER
'What I've learned from Tantra is that sex is another way of getting into a powerful and connected state, and when you feel that good, life becomes a lot easier.'

WHERE DOES TANTRA COME FROM?

Tantra originated in India more than 5000 years ago as a quiet rebellion against a male priesthood which had decided that sexuality must be repressed for an individual to reach enlightenment. The first Tantrics were men and women teachers who felt that sexuality was a gift of the Divine and should be celebrated. They also believed that the experience of good sex offered ordinary people glimpses of love that could be explored as part of their spiritual development.

Even today in the West, where sex plays little part in organized religion, there are times when people feel that making love can take them out of themselves and unite them with their partner in a unique way. They may even be aware of a deeper sense of connection with the universe or God as a result. Most of us, however, have only an occasional glimmer of this bigger picture. The Tantric teachers created practices that enable anyone with a willing spirit and an open mind to access this potent energy whenever they feel ready. Tantra shows you simple steps to sexual ecstasy.

IS TANTRA A RELIGION?

Tantra is essentially an Eastern spiritual practice. But it is not a religion and anyone can do it. You don't have to be vegetarian and you don't have to be wacky. Window cleaners, management consultants, teachers and lawyers all practise Tantra.

It is perfectly possible for you to follow your own spiritual beliefs and to practise Tantra as well. Tantra does not have long lists of rules, and the exercises outlined in this book embrace both heterosexual and homosexual relationships. The balance between male and female is important within Tantra, but it is a polarity that we need to examine within ourselves as well as in our relationships with others. By exploring their inner male energy, instead of ignoring or denying it, for example, women are better able to connect to their femininity. Equally, when men are able to acknowledge their vulnerability, which is usually seen as a feminine trait, they gain a clearer and healthier sense of their masculinity. Only when we can move beyond our narrow preconceptions of gender can we embrace the fundamental nature of our own sex, and lead fuller and happier lives as a result.

BASIC TANTRA FACTS

Tantra does not focus on who you make love with, but, rather, on how you make love. In Tantric sex, you respect and appreciate your partner as the other half of yourself. You honour each other with love and tenderness.

Tantra teaches you how to enjoy sexual excitement without tension. Instead of succumbing to a rising spiral of excitement that peaks with a few brief seconds of orgasm, Tantra enables you to move this sexual energy around your body, even to store it in your body, and to relax into a series of peaks of excitement. (When you experience a surge of internal excitement on meeting someone you find very attractive, that's an example of sexual energy.) Tantra can help women who don't have orgasms to become orgasmic. And it can enable men to be multi-orgasmic for virtually as long as they like.

BERNADETTE, 31, TEACHER

'When a normal orgasm is over, you might feel a bit tingly afterwards, but that's it. The sensation is mostly in the genitals. When I have a Tantric experience, the energy circulates around my body and I can orgasm countless times; it is like ripples going on and on. In Tantra, the whole body is involved and you can store the energy when you feel you've had enough, or you can simply open up to deeper realms of bliss. Sometimes you have insights into the nature of existence itself; a sense of the underlying unity of things.'

From a Western perspective, the most revolutionary aspect of Tantric sex is that male orgasm and ejaculation are not inextricably linked. A man can control his ability to ejaculate and can experience full-body orgasms without ejaculation. This means that he can become as multi-orgasmic as a woman. Yes, this is possible, and it is a great deal easier than you might think. And it gets even better. You can learn how to circulate your sexual energy throughout your body. If you are a man, imagine making love and feeling full of energy afterwards, instead of feeling tired or even wiped out. Sound appealing? Tantra shows you how sex can give you energy rather than drain you of it.

Mike, 42, management consultant
'If I'd had to rate a genital orgasm before, I'd have given it a nine out of ten. Now I have experienced a full-body orgasm, I would probably rate a genital orgasm at about six. But I'd give a full-body orgasm ten out of ten. If someone asked me to sum it up, I'd say 'Bloody amazing!'

It may be a cliché to say that sex is everywhere, but we are bombarded by sexual images in advertising, magazines and movies. Yet for many of us sexual bliss is not part of our reality. It's like a distant island that hovers on the horizon. We remain stranded on the shoreline, gazing out to sea and feeling as if we've missed the boat. Tantra gives you the tickets to get there.

And while sex may fascinate most of us, it's worth remembering that almost all sexual acts can be painful, unpleasant or just dull unless you do them with someone who turns you on. Tantra teaches you to flick the switch of sexual desire whenever you want.

A word about language

The Tantras were written texts describing sexual and social practices which have been passed down through the centuries. They were written in Sanskrit, which is the Indian equivalent of Latin, and many Sanskrit terms are still used in Tantra today. Modern Tantric teachers, for example, often use the terms 'Shiva' and 'Shakti' when referring to the male and female to help students focus on the divine god or goddess aspect within. It is a kind of shorthand for seeing a different and unfamiliar side of yourself. They also use the Sanskrit words for the genitals, notably *vajra* or *lingham* for penis, and *yoni* for vagina, both of which are definitely softer and less clinical than their English equivalents.

In Tantra the word yoni means 'sacred place'. Yoni is respected as the source of universal bliss. It is considerably different from the modern English slang words for female genitals that are also used as terms of abuse. Vajra means 'tool of consciousness' and again has rather more majestic connotations than our colloquial terms of 'cock' or 'dick', which are also embedded in our consciousness as insults.

RACHEL, 34, LECTURER

'Most of the sexual words we use in the West are clinical, ugly or vulgar. I loved finding words for penis and vagina that really appealed to me. Vajra and yoni sound respectful and honouring. The words seem to represent what they are so much better than the Anglo-Saxon terminology. It's like having a new language that I can use without sounding awkward or embarrassed.'

JAMES, 45, ELECTRICIAN

'At first I found the language totally weird. I thought, "What's wrong with 'penis' and 'fuck?' " But then I discovered that vajra means "tool of consciousness" and I really like that. I started to do Tantra workshops and I suppose I got gradually acclimatised to the language. Now if my kids talk to me about a sexual problem I actually find it hard to say "penis" and not vajra.'

You may feel you are perfectly happy with the words you already use. If, on the other hand, you have always found something faintly dispiriting about the English slang for genitals, vajra and yoni are appealing alternatives.

THE TAO

As ancient Tantric practices spread to China, they became assimilated into another philosophy, the Tao, which literally means 'The Way'. Traditional Chinese culture formed around the Tao, which still forms the basis for practically everything from medicine to cookery. Acupuncture, Chinese herbal remedies and more recently Feng Shui are just three of the healing arts that originated in ancient China and are now hugely popular in the West.

Taoists (pronounced 'Dowists') have much in common with people who practise Tantra. Both Tantra and the Tao believe that sexual energy runs through the body from head to toe through a series of pathways, or 'meridians', and that this energy is a powerful life force. They agree that multiple orgasms are perfectly accessible to both sexes; that women can ejaculate as well as men; that orgasm can happen to women and men without ejaculation; and that orgasm can lead to an altered state of consciousness.

As Tantra and the Tao share so much, I have included exercises from both, and I've spoken to dozens of men and women and included their thoughts − both light-hearted and serious − in this book. Some of these interviewees have been interested in Tantra and the Tao for just a few months; others have been involved for most of their adult lives.

If you are interested in deepening your current relationship, finding out more about your sexuality or simply picking up some great tips to rev up your sex life, Tantra deserves to be explored.

1

ENERGY IS
ETERNAL DELIGHT

Tantra is about the flow and exchange of energy – the movement of life. Tantrics believe that the most powerful energy is sexual energy. Tantric practice shows you how to circulate this energy around your own body and then move it between you and your partner. You will discover how to take the sexual feelings you have in your genitals and to move them up to different areas of your body and ultimately to your brain, where they are experienced as ecstasy. As this energy moves through your body, it sets off fireworks en route.

What Westerners think of as getting 'turned on' or 'horny', Tantrics and Taoists think of as generating sexual energy. You can be in touch with this powerful energy all the time. But you'll probably be glad to know that this does not result in feeling unbearably aroused 24 hours a day. Tantra teaches you how to have access to this energy and how to store it in your body. So, instead of being subject to uncontrollable sexual urges, you feel more creative, more alive and more in touch

'When you learn to move sexual energy away from the genitals into the rest of your body, the word "sexual" somehow becomes irrelevant because the experience becomes different. But by doing this we find the things that we search for in our sexuality – a sense of being very alive, and feelings of excitement, contact and connection.'

with your senses as you go about your daily life. You can shop, work, play and get fit with a spring in your step and a positive sense of wellbeing.

In the West we tend to think the only way we can get in touch with our sexual energy is through someone else. Couples in tired marriages, for example, may feel tempted by an affair that will make them feel 'alive' again. Meeting someone new is certainly one way of accessing that giddy and exciting sense of 'being in love' – but it is not the only way. Tantra teaches us that the powerful sexual energy that we think can only be ignited by another person *exists in us all the time*. And we can learn how to channel it for ourselves.

Tantra teacher John explains: 'When you learn to move sexual energy away from the genitals into the rest of your body, the word "sexual" somehow becomes irrelevant because the experience becomes different. But by doing this we find the things that we search for in our sexuality – a sense of being very alive, and feelings of excitement, contact and connection.'

As the poet William Blake wrote, 'Energy is eternal delight.'

SO WHAT IS ENERGY?

You can't see energy but you can feel it. We are all energetic beings. We are made of atoms that have vibrating movements and rhythms. Our hearts pulsate, our diaphragms move as we breathe and our lungs pump air in and out of the body. We belong to a universe that hums with energy and we are part of those vibrations.

Chinese medicine, for example, works on the principle that when energy flow in the body becomes blocked the result is illness. For acupuncture practitioners there is no doubt about the role of chi, or the life-force in the body. They insert very fine metal needles into the skin at any of 800 specially designated points in order to manipulate the body's chi and allow the body to re-balance and heal itself.

Some people find that through Tantra they become highly attuned to energy in their bodies:

Wayne, 34, antiques restorer

'It's possible to feel your own energy passing up your spine and down the front of your body, and then up your partner's spine and down the front of her body in a continual loop between you. It's a process of connection that I find very beautiful. For me it feels like an electrical fire; it is warm and from time to time it gets hot. When it gets into my brain it can feel like a blazing light and you can see things. Some people experience visions. I just get flashes of light, but it is still fantastic.'

Boosting your energy

If at times you feel tired and lethargic, there are some pretty straightforward ways of giving yourself an instant energy boost. Instead of opting for a strong coffee to wake you up, try breathing deeply to increase your intake of oxygen, so that your belly expands as you fill your lungs. Take up to seven deep breaths in and out, then revert to normal breathing, and continue this pattern until you start to feel your body kick-start into action. (Breathing deeply for too long when you are unaccustomed to it will make you feel dizzy, so stop and breathe normally if you begin to feel light-headed).

Alternatively, start to move; ideally to dance or run. Energy is blocked when you slump onto the sofa and released when your body and limbs begin to move. Experience a double whammy with the addition of sound, another positive source of energy, by putting on a CD that makes you want to dance. If you have young children, dance with them; they are always ready to strut their stuff. If you live alone, seize the opportunity to dance as wildly as you like; no one is watching, so no one can laugh. (Draw the curtains if you have nosy neighbours). If you are dubious about the benefits of dancing, just think about why people dance when they go partner-hunting at parties. Dancing has been described as 'the vertical expression of a horizontal desire' and when you dance with someone you find attractive, you are actually stirring up sexual energy in your body, ready to use later.

Get dancing and within minutes you will feel more awake and you will find your brain is less sluggish. If you are someone who is uncomfortable with the idea of dancing either publicly or in private, resolve to give it another try without judging yourself while you do it. If you still find the idea of dancing about as appealing as an hors d'oeuvres of Pedigree Chum, run on the spot or do a few bends and stretches instead.

Still uncertain what energy feels like? Try this experiment. Vigorously shake your right hand for a minute or so. When you stop and hold it in front of you, bring your left hand, palms facing, gently towards it, and you should feel a vibrating sensation around the hand that has been shaken. It may feel pleasantly buzzy and warm, or it may even feel larger than the unshaken hand.

By shaking your hand you have charged it with energy and if you place your attention there you will feel it. One of the things that Tantra does is to teach you how to generate and move this warm, tingly energy throughout your body.

THE CHAKRAS

According to Tantra, there are seven principal energy centres inside the body through which the energy can flow. These are called the chakras. Chakra is the Sanskrit word for 'wheel'. The chakras run in a straight line from the perineum (the area between the anus and the genitals) to the top of the head. They are like internal power stations, creating and maintaining energy. Scientifically, they correspond to the endocrine system, which governs hormonal secretion and keeps the body balanced.

According to Western medicine, seven glands regulate the body's vitality and energy flow. These are the sex glands; the adrenals; the pancreas; the thymus; the thyroid; the pituitary and the pineal glands. Eastern culture suggests that the chakras, the corresponding energy centres linked to these glands, also relate to aspects of the personality. In the words of B.K.S. Iyengar, a modern Indian teacher of Hatha yoga: 'As antennae pick up radio waves and transform them into sound through receiving sets, chakras pick up cosmic vibrations and distribute them throughout the body.'

So the emotions you experience can translate into a physical sensation. If you are feeling fearful or anxious, the fear will manifest itself in your body and you may feel 'butterflies' in your stomach. Equally, if you feel very emotional but can't find

the words to say anything, it can bring a 'lump' to your throat. These are common sensations associated with the chakras which most of us have felt at one time or another. Like electricity, the chakras cannot be seen, but in the same way that you can switch on a light and illuminate a room, their effects can be witnessed.

Broadly speaking, the seven main chakras are recognised as the base or root chakra (which lies at the perineum); the sacral (located roughly 5cm [2 in] below the navel); the solar plexus (in the central hollow of the stomach); the heart (in the centre of the chest, midway between the nipples); the throat; the forehead, or 'third eye' (in the forehead between the eyebrows), and the crown chakra (at the top of the head). It helps some people to imagine them as gently rotating wheels of light, each about 5 cm (2 in) in diameter.

THE SEVEN CHAKRAS

crown

forehead *(3rd eye)*

throat

heart

solar plexus

sacral

root

Martial arts students have long used the principle of the chakras in their disciplines. They believe that the sacral chakra, located just under the navel, is the body's natural centre of balance. In China it is called the tan tien and in Japan the hara, and it is believed to be a source of gravity and strength.

The colours used to represent the chakras visually are the colours of the rainbow; red for the root, orange for the sacral; yellow for the solar plexus; green (or pink) for the heart; blue for the throat; indigo for the forehead and violet (or pure white) for the crown.

ENERGY AND EMOTIONS

According to Tantra teacher Leora, the chakras have specific links to our emotions. She says: 'The base chakra corresponds to the basic life force energy. It relates to our connection to the earth and to the planet. It is about survival. If it is closed you will probably feel a chronic sense of fear and unsafety. People feel they are under threat – that they might get some awful disease or that an accident will happen; that the world is against them.' When the energy is flowing freely through this chakra, you feel that life supports you whatever you do. Equally your sex life is grounded and complete. You feel connected to Nature and that the world is a friendly place.

The emotions connected with the remaining chakras are as follows:

The sacral chakra is the creative and sexual centre, where the basic life-force is transformed into humanity. When the energy is fully released in this chakra, you feel strength, vitality and a sense of aliveness that comes from a healthy, relaxed body. It is also where you get your gut instincts from. If this chakra is open, you are more in touch with this feeling of creativity. When closed, however, it's a different story. The flow of sexual energy is reduced and people can feel stiff, tense and critical. There may be a reluctance to have sex or it may not be fully integrated with the rest of their body and mind; it will be more like a purely physical function.

The solar plexus chakra is connected with identity, says Leora: 'It's about our individual identity within our tribe and our power in the sense of who we are and

Love is one of our basic human needs, and when we lack it we can lose our sense of purpose in life. If you can keep the heart chakra open, you may experience pain, but that is something you can accept and let go, rather than shutting down in the face of it what we mean. It's also the point where we manifest our creativity. Some people are very creative but if this chakra is closed, they never get to the point where they share it with the world. When this chakra is open, both partners feel as if they are masters of their emotions and capable of being equal partners. When it is blocked, sex feels threatening. There may be difficulty letting go and receiving.'

The heart chakra is the connection between the lower and higher chakras. When open, it gives us the sense of being in love. We tend to think that being in love depends on the one we are in love with, but Tantra is about finding our way to experience this sense of love for ourselves. When the heart chakra is closed, you feel cut off and closed. You may want to protect yourself from pain, but you can't feel love either. There is a sense of not wanting to be vulnerable or to commit. It can be a very lonely place.

Love is one of our basic human needs, and when we lack it we can lose our sense of purpose in life. If you can keep the heart chakra open, you may experience pain, but that is something you can accept and let go, rather than shutting down in the face of it. If the heart is open there will, inevitably, be joy and sadness. But your life will be richer. An open heart chakra leads you to an understanding that joy and sadness are not necessarily two distinct places but, rather, are part of the same circle. When you recognize this, you will be better able to cope with both.

The throat chakra is connected with communication. An open throat chakra allows you to express yourself freely and is about being heard. If we bite our lip and don't say what we mean, this can manifest by blocking the throat chakra and we often live with resentment as a result.

The forehead chakra relates to insight, intuition, clarity and vision. It lies in the centre of the face, between and behind the eyebrows. In the East, this area is known as the third eye. When it is closed, people rely too much on logic and on the brain, and may have difficulty making decisions. This can lead to an overdependence on other people as we don't have an 'inner sense' ourselves. It becomes hard to see the magic in life.

The crown chakra is a place of connection with the bigger picture. According to Leora: 'Sometimes people from religious backgrounds will have some kind of block in this chakra because they may have had negative experiences with religion that they will equate with spirituality. Also, people who are naturally spiritual can have been silenced as children because those qualities haven't been received well in their families. If this is closed, it is all about "me, here, now". There is nothing more than that.' For some people this crown chakra represents their connection with God or the Divine; for others it is about their link to the rest of the universe.

If you find these ideas hard to digest, the story below is a good illustration of the way the chakras and energy flow can affect the body:

COLIN, 51, MANAGEMENT TRAINER

'The first time I was asked to imagine energy flowing in my body on a Tantra holiday workshop, I felt absolutely zero. Then I listened to a talk about the chakras and it was the first time I had come across a description of what they are about. We moved on to doing a chakra massage with our partners and as my wife began to move her hands over me I began to see waves and different colours and shapes. When she reached my solar plexus everything went haywire. I felt completely calm in the upper part of my body, but everything else went into turmoil. My arms and legs became spread-eagled to the four points on the ground and I couldn't move.

I was an engineer and the only way I can describe it was that I needed two people to create an electrical circuit between the two parts of my body like a plug and socket. They had to create a connection. I told them to hold my thumbs and toes as what I can only describe as an electrical force pinned me flat to the floor. It was like being sucked towards the floor by a magnet. It wasn't painful, but I couldn't move. I can't remember how long this lasted, but suddenly it stopped and everything went into complete relaxation. My eyes were closed, but I felt I was looking upwards into a shaft of light. I also knew that I was firmly attached to the earth.

At no point did I feel frightened. It was an enthralling and fascinating experience. I was in total bliss, a state of complete tranquillity. At the end of the exercise, I couldn't move very easily for two or three minutes. I wasn't shaking, I just had to come back to earth and to get all my muscles moving again. In a very short while I was able to be normal again, but the overall effect of it was quite mind-blowing.

When I went back to work after the holiday, my colleagues could see that something had happened because I was quite different. I was a changed person, entirely for the better. I was much more relaxed, more able to cope with whatever life threw at me and to focus on and handle problems. I'd been away for a week, but I felt as if I had been on holiday for a month and I was completely OK about going back to work. I was even able to see the Human Resources department and ask if I was going to be made redundant and when they said yes I stayed fine about it.

I had no idea that energy could have such an impact on your everyday life. That realisation has had a profound effect on me.'

WE ARE ALL CONNECTED

Not only do chakras work inside our own bodies, they also resonate with the chakras in the other people we meet. Which is why we feel in harmony with some individuals and ill at ease with others. You may know people whom you can practically guarantee will give you a boost, while others will almost inevitably drag you down. This isn't imaginary; it is a very real effect of the way energy flows between people.

KUNDALINI ENERGY

Tantrics believe there is a powerful energy, known as Kundalini energy, which lies dormant at the base of the spine. Tantric drawings represent this as a coiled snake. If awakened, it shoots straight up the body to the brain. This is accompanied by an intense sensation of joy, a feeling of being cleansed and also deeply relaxed. You can get in touch with this energy through a number of routes, including meditation and yoga. Another way is through Tantric sex.

Teachers of Kundalini yoga describe their path as a way of reaching our latent potential and expanding our consciousness and vision. In their understanding, as the energy uncoils, it rises from the base of the body to the crown of the head and leads to a change in awareness. On the return journey it brings enlightenment.

Kundalini energy is not something you need to manufacture; it is already there,

ROGER,

47, SALESMAN

*'I am very down to earth and I
can't really relate to the chakras
and the energy stuff, but I do
believe that people have got energy
stored inside them. The first time I
practised streaming energy through
pelvic bouncing, it was a total
release for me.'*

Visualisation, or picturing images in your head to help you achieve a positive goal, is a useful tool that is becoming increasingly popular with a wide range of people from sales managers to cancer patients. Top athletes use it all the time to help them meet and then surpass their mental and physical targets. The theory behind it is that the brain programmes and re-programmes itself through its images. Visualisation is a useful technique for improving sexual relationships, and it is well worth giving it a try.

waiting to be discovered. In Tantra, preparation for sex involves channelling this energy through the body, so that you and your lover may experience it flowing freely between you, bringing intense emotions of joy and intimacy.

There are many myths and even scare stories surrounding the potency of Kundalini energy. As with any physical or mental practices, use common sense and be guided by your own response. According to Tantra teacher Leora: 'The exercises that we do in Tantra with Kundalini energy are entirely beneficial. We aim to softly release tension to allow the energy to flow through the body. We practise something called "streaming", which is like gently washing away the debris that collects in a river in order to allow the river to move freely.'

It is quite simple to experience this energy for yourself. Pelvic bouncing, when you lie on your back (and yes, you've guessed), bounce your pelvis up and down, is an exercise that can produce surprisingly powerful results. Try this:

PELVIC BOUNCING

Make yourself comfortable and lie on your back, either on a soft quilt or cushions or on the floor – whichever you prefer.

Rest your arms by your sides, palms facing upwards. Bend your knees and plant your feet flat on the floor, your hips' width apart. Lengthen your neck and relax your jaw and shoulders. Keep your neck relaxed as you start to raise your pelvis from the floor. Begin to bounce your pelvis up and down; you can either do this rhythmically, or you can experiment with different speeds. It may feel like hard work at first, but don't be put off. (A musical soundtrack with a strong beat will help.)

The first time I tried this, I felt like giving up after a couple of minutes. Then it started to feel as though the bouncing was taking me over and it became pretty much effortless. When bouncing, you are in effect charging the whole of your body with energy. When you stop, the energy will start to move upwards. It may make it easier if you imagine it as a silver or gold light moving up to the top of your head and then tracing a line down the front of your body to settle in your navel.

ROGER, 47, COMPANY DIRECTOR

'I am very down to earth and I can't really relate to the chakras and the energy stuff, but I do believe that people have got energy stored inside them. The first time I practised streaming energy through pelvic bouncing, it was a total release for me. I haven't a clue how it works, other than I have a total willingness to do it. I love it. I feel totally in control but I shake and cry during it. I think my wife got a bit concerned the first time I did it, but I think it is absolutely fantastic and the best thing is that I feel wonderful afterwards.'

EXPLORING YOUR ENERGY

The best way to become more familiar with the concept of energy moving inside your body is to experiment. Tantra teacher Margo Anand calls the process of moving energy up through the chakras experiencing 'the inner flute'. When I first heard this, I couldn't help wondering where the rest of the 'inner orchestra' had gone, but sometimes you have to put your cynicism to one side and accept that this is simply a metaphor to make a practice, which requires a degree of imagination, easier. Here are some things you can try:

VISUALISATION

Visualisation, or picturing images in your head to help you achieve a positive goal, is a useful tool that is becoming increasingly popular with a wide range of people from sales managers to cancer patients. Top athletes use it all the time to help them meet and then surpass their mental and physical targets. The theory behind it is that the brain programmes and re-programmes itself through its images. Visualisation is a useful technique for improving sexual relationships, and it is well worth giving it a try.

All you have to do is find somewhere comfortable and quiet, where you won't be disturbed for 10 minutes or so, lie on your back and breathe in and out. As you do so, contract and release the pubococcygeus (PC) muscle (that's the one you use when you are desperate to go to the loo, but need to hold on). This can be done by men and women. (More information about the PC muscle, and how it works, is given in Chapter Two on pages 48 & 59.)

If you
would like
to enjoy
**something a little
more dramatic**, try
the Cherokee
Chuluaqui
Quodoushka teaching
known as the **Firebreath
Orgasm**, which will
enable you to
experience an orgasm
fully clothed and
without any genital
stimulation
(honestly!)

As you contract this muscle, breathe in and imagine the breath moving up through your body to the crown of your head. Breathe out and feel the breath flowing outwards as you release your PC muscle. It may help if you gently trace its progress with your left or right hand as you imagine it moving inside you. Don't be discouraged if you don't feel anything at all at first. It takes time to become sensitive to the movement of energy, but it is worth persevering because this is a valuable technique to take with you into Tantric sex.

In Tantric texts the chakras are usually depicted as lotus flowers. If you are a newcomer to the idea of the chakras, try this exercise to open them up and help the energy to flow more freely in your body:

Sit or lie so that you are comfortable; slowly move your attention from each chakra to the next, imagining, as you do so, a flower of the relevant chakra colour opening its petals from a bud into full bloom. Breathe deeply and relax. Allow yourself at least 10 minutes' peace in order to do this. Again, don't worry if you can't feel anything much immediately. Focus on something that does work (even if it feels very small) rather than dwelling on what isn't working. Keep going and slowly you will become more in tune with the energy in your body.

THE FIREBREATH ORGASM

If you would like to enjoy something a little more dramatic, try the Cherokee Chuluaqui Quodoushka teaching known as the Firebreath Orgasm, which will enable you to experience an orgasm fully clothed and without any genital stimulation. (Honestly!)

Lie on your back with your knees up, as though you were going to begin pelvic bouncing. In this exercise, and unusually for Tantric practice, you breathe through your mouth. Imagine drawing energy (think of it as gold or silver light, if this helps) from your base chakra, tightening your PC muscle (see Chapter Two, pages 48 & 59) with each inhalation. Then breathe the energy (or coloured light) up to the sacral chakra – it might help to draw your hand up and down your body as you do this. Repeat this process between the sacral and solar plexus chakras, and then the solar plexus and heart chakras. Continue breathing energy up into the throat, third eye and finally the crown.

When you get to the crown (or sometimes way before) you may find that you have started to shake or your back is arching. Don't be alarmed – you are simply experiencing the energy flow through your body. You should also be feeling good. Just go with it. When you are ready, start to bring the energy back down to your navel area and relax as deeply as you can. You may feel extremely calm and centred afterwards. Enjoy the feeling for as long as it lasts.

A fun exercise for two...

If you feel that exploring energy would be more fun to do with a partner, there is a pleasurable way to make it feel more like play and less like homework. Cuddle together like spoons – both on the same side with one partner cradling the other – or one sitting immediately in front of the other, and breathe in unison. If the man is lying behind the woman, he should place his hand over hers and you should both breathe in and out into each chakra, so you start at the base of the body and slowly work your way up through the navel, solar plexus, heart, throat, forehead and crown. Just be aware of any sensations you experience; you may feel a warmth or tingling where you rest your hands. You don't have to speak to your partner while you do this, just relax as deeply as you can. If you take your time, and do this exercise properly, you should begin to notice a difference in the quality of your sexual relationship almost immediately.

Some Tantric short cuts

If all this talk of exercises is starting to sound a little daunting you might like to try one of these short cuts. You can do them separately or together.

The next time you experience an orgasm, just imagine energy moving around your body, away from the genital region. You don't have to do anything complicated, like trying to move it physically or force it in another direction, just relax and imagine it lightly moving up your spine.

Keep the tip of your tongue on the roof of your mouth, at the front of the palate. This will help the energy circulate (exactly how this works will be explained later). It is relatively easy to do and a simple first step on a path where you recognize that sexual energy need not be confined to a restricted area of the body.

The next time you make love, breathe deeply as you approach orgasm. Most people tend to hold their breath, tighten up and 'will' their orgasm to happen. In reality, your orgasm will be more intense if you can relax into it and breathe deeply and fully.

A final note about energy. According to ancient Tantric texts, the god Shiva embodied consciousness and his consort, Shakti, was the embodiment of pure energy. By uniting spiritually and sexually with Shiva, Shakti gave form to his spirit and created the universe. You don't have to believe this story to practise Tantra, but I rather like the idea that our energy-filled universe was created as an act of erotic love.

2

BODIES, BRAINS AND BELIEFS

In the West we like to think we have a sophisticated attitude towards our bodies. Some people count calories or try different diets to lose weight, others opt for surgery to change the shape of their features or to look younger. And even if you are not one of the thousands of people who work out in a gym for a better physique, the chances are that you will have given your physical appearance more than a passing thought.

But while newspapers and magazines may be obsessed with the flatness of a certain pop star's stomach, or the breast implants of a Hollywood actress, many of us remain ignorant about the way our own bodies work, especially in relation to our sexual responses. This is partly because very few of us have ever been taught about sexual anatomy. If you are a woman, even if you paid careful attention during your biology classes as school, the chances are that no one told you precisely where the G-spot is on the vagina … let alone how best to stimulate it. If you are a man, can you say that you know exactly where one of a male's most sensitive sexual places is? (Here's a clue…it's not on your penis.)

If you are to experience Tantra fully, you will find it helpful to understand your body and your own sexual responses, as well as those of your partner. The fact is, a huge number of men know more about the internal workings of their car than those of their wife or girlfriend. Equally, there are plenty of women who regard male sexual apparatus as an unsightly blot on the landscape and make little attempt to understand its sensitive and sensual nature.

If you are fully confident that you know how male and female sexual equipment works, try answering the following questions:

- Some women ejaculate when they reach orgasm – true or false?
- Some women have more nerve endings in the labia minora (inner lips) than in the clitoris – true or false?
- The first third of the vagina is more sensitive to touch, while the back two-thirds are more sensitive to pressure – true or false?
- Changing hormone levels can affect a man's mood. Some men become irritable or depressed when their testosterone level rises – true or false?

All of the above statements are true. If you knew this, congratulations – you are far better informed than most people and you may like to skip this chapter. If, however, you weren't absolutely certain of every answer, it could be worthwhile reading on.

CORINNE, 44, CIVIL SERVANT
'I feel embarrassed to admit it, but despite having had two children there was still lots of information about my body that I didn't know until I discovered Tantra. For me, Tantra is sex education for grown-ups.'

This isn't a science book; it's a book about creating pleasure. As a result I haven't included biological line drawings that are rarely fun or sexy to look at but instead have opted for very simple descriptions. If you are a woman and want to check out the penis in detail, look carefully (and lovingly) at your partner (with his permission, naturally). If you are a man wanting to find out more about a woman, do likewise. If you are single, there are plenty of other books that will give you detailed pictures of male and female sexual anatomy, some of which are listed in the Further Reading section. Equally, both sexes can explore their own bodies, with the use of a mirror and, if necessary, a small torch. (Apologies if that sounds like a check-list for scout camp.)

THE INTIMATE GEOGRAPHY OF A WOMAN

The most important fact to remember when considering female sexual anatomy is that every woman is different. Some text books confidently assert that all women are designed in the same way – they are not. In the late 1950s, a scientist called Kermit Krantz explored the link between women's genitals and their nervous system. Krantz discovered that there was a wide variation in the way nerve endings were distributed throughout different women. Although most women had a higher concentration of nerve endings in the clitoris, some had more nerve endings in the labia minora (inner lips). Similarly, some women's nerve endings were highly concentrated in one part of the body, while others had nerve endings spread out

Men need to think twice before they stimulate their new partner in the same way that used to drive a former lover wild. (It could be about as effective as calling her by their ex-girlfriend's name.) And for women there is a responsibility to tell their partner what they like and dislike over a wider area. In other words, no two women get turned on sexually in the same way.

This is a useful fact for their partners to remember. For men, what one girlfriend may have loved another will hate. Men need to think twice before they stimulate their new partner in the same way that used to drive a former lover wild. (It could be about as effective as calling her by their ex-girlfriend's name.) And for women there is a responsibility to tell their partner what they like and dislike. Don't expect a man to know his way around without a mental map. It is a journey he has never made before.

As each woman responds differently sexually, so each has genitals that are unique to her – just as no two faces look exactly alike. In Tantra, a woman's genitals are known as her yoni. It is here that a woman's most powerful energy resides. In Sanskrit, yoni means 'womb' or 'sacred place', but in Tantric common usage, yoni has come to refer to the vulva, which consists of different areas: the outer lips (labia majora); the inner lips (labia minora) and the clitoral hood; the tip or glans of the clitoris (if it can be seen through the clitoral hood); the urethral opening; the opening of the vagina; and the mons pubis (a fleshy little mound on top of the pubic bone, usually covered by pubic hair).

THE OUTER AND INNER LIPS

The outer lips of the vulva are often covered in hair, while the inner lips are smooth as silk. They also tend to be more sensitive, partly because they are connected to the hood of the clitoris. They often swell and change colour (usually to a deep reddish-purple) when aroused.

It was the Romans who named the outer lips of the vulva the 'labia majora' (big lips) and the inner lips the 'labia minora'. But despite their great road-building skills and their innovative central heating systems, when it came to women the Romans got it wrong. In a lot of women, the outer lips are not particularly noticeable; it is the inner lips that can be seen more readily. The labia majora, though, do serve a vital function. They secrete fluids for lubrication during sexual arousal. But you don't have to rely on them.

At various stages in a woman's menstrual cycle, and especially during and after the menopause, they don't work quite so effectively, and this is the time to reach for a water-based vaginal lubricant from the chemist's counter. There are plenty of these available, and it is worth trying a few to find the one that is best for you. Never use Vaseline (petroleum jelly) inside your vagina, however, as it blocks the vagina's ability to cleanse itself and may result in infections.

Equally, steer clear of using oil-based lubricants (such as massage oil), either on their own or in conjunction with latex condoms. Oil-based products will damage latex in less than 60 seconds. KY jelly may not be particularly hip, but it is one of the cheapest and best regarded medically. Plus, you can usually pick it up with your weekly supermarket shop. Using a lubricant during sex doesn't make you any less of a woman; it simply makes you an organised woman.

THE CLITORIS

One of my favourite moments from Willy Russell's award-winning stage play, *Shirley Valentine*, is when his heroine mulls over the word 'clitoris'. She decides that it sounds like a rather nice girl's name: 'Clitoris, come in for your tea.' How you pronounce it depends on the speaker. Some people prefer CLIToris, others say clitORis, (to rhyme with Doris). The first is the more usual. As for a definition of what it is, I like Eve Ensler's quotation in her performance of *The Vagina Monologues*, from Natalie Angier's *Woman: An Intimate Geography*. It is this:

The clitoris is pure in purpose. It is the only organ in the body designed purely for pleasure. The clitoris is simply a bundle of nerves: 8,000 nerve fibres, to be precise. That's a higher concentration of nerve fibres than is found anywhere else in the body, including the fingertips, lips and tongue, and it is twice … twice … twice the number in the penis. Who needs a handgun when you've got a semiautomatic.

Some clitorises like to be rubbed and sucked; others can hardly stand to be breathed upon. In that case, it can be more effective for a partner to stroke the connecting inner lips of the vulva. The size of a clitoris ranges from 2 to 20 mm in diameter. As a woman becomes aroused, the tip of her clitoris often swells. Medical opinion used to believe that as far as the clitoris was concerned, what you saw was what you got. But recently, research has shown that the clitoris is a far larger organ than was once thought. It was not until 1998 that a female urologist discovered that the clitoris is twice as large and far more anatomically complex than described in most medical textbooks.

Tantra teaches that women have a subtle nerve connecting their clitoris to their upper lip. The Kama Sutra suggests that the man nibble or suck her upper lip while she kisses his lower lip. This idea extends beyond India. In Japan, shiatsu massage links the upper lip to the digestive and sexual system and considers that pressure here stimulates sexual desire. Try it with your partner and see what happens.

THE URETHRAL OPENING

This can be as hard to locate as a mink coat in a vegetarian's wardrobe. But although its function (to allow urine to pass out of the body) seems mundane, albeit necessary, it doesn't miss out on enjoying a large number of nerve endings that are supremely sensitive to touch. The entrance to the urethra is surrounded by an acorn-shaped, protruding edge called the glans. During lovemaking, this is pressed between the penis of the man and the woman's pubic bone – it can be painful or pleasurable, depending on the sensitivity and quality of what's going on between the couple.

Some women, when extremely aroused, may panic because they think they are going to urinate. This won't happen but their panic is understandable. The feeling is due to an area along the floor of the urethral channel (which is the 'ceiling' of the vagina) inhabited by the Bartholin ducts, which are also known as the female prostatic glands. This area on the roof of the vagina feels ridged, whereas the side-walls of the vagina are smooth.

During sexual excitement, a concentration of blood vessels around the urethra, known as the urethral sponge, swells with blood and this can be felt inside the vagina (about a third to three-quarters of a finger deep). If you have ever heard of the G-spot and wondered what it is (Goodtime spot, perhaps?) here is your answer.

THE G-SPOT

Named after Ernest Grafenberg, the German gynaecologist who discovered it (in terms of medical history only; presumably millions of women knew about it before he did), the G-spot swells during sexual arousal and presses against the wall of the vagina. If you want to find it, try inserting a finger into the vagina and making a 'Come here' motion. The best position for stimulating the G-spot during lovemaking is when you sit, lie on your front, kneel for rear entry, or make love on top of your male partner.

When a woman is very aroused, she may experience an orgasm accompanied by the expulsion of a clear fluid from the G-spot through the urethra. This is not urine, but a mixture of several fluids, including vaginal secretions, secretions from the Bartholin ducts and mucus from the cervix at the top of the vagina. We know it is not urine, because one researcher gave women a drink that turned their urine blue, and the ejaculation from their G-spot was not blue. (I always wonder just how these researchers persuade people to take part in their experiments …)

The quantity of fluid that a woman may ejaculate can vary from very little to quite a lot – enough to make you feel that you have urinated. If this is the case, don't worry. Simply relax and enjoy the wonderful sensation. If you feel protective towards your bedlinen/carpet/stripped wooden floor, put a towel underneath you beforehand.

Interestingly, until the last couple of decades, many doctors denied the existence of female ejaculation. But Vatsyayana, author of the Kama Sutra, was aware of it. He wrote: 'The semen of women continues to fall from the beginning of the sexual union to its end, in the same way as that of the male.' The Tantric Buddhists also promoted the mixing of male and female sexual fluids. Their texts rather poetically refer to a woman's madhu, meaning something sweet like honey, nectar or wine.

An added talent of the G-spot is its ability to transmit sensations to the brain through the pelvic nerve (the same nerve that transmits bladder sensations). Sensations produced by clitoral stimulation are sent by way of the pudendal nerve, which is linked to the spinal cord. Dr John Perry and Dr Beverly Whipple, medical authorities on the G-spot, are adamant that women's orgasms are transmitted to the brain by both these neural pathways, rather than just one. If this is the case, it does explain why a large percentage of women who have spinal-cord injuries are still able to have genital orgasms. The chances are that there must be a secondary pathway to the brain for orgasms besides the one that runs up the spinal column.

THE VAGINA

The vagina is a hollow canal with walls that contain nerves and blood vessels. When unaroused, the walls lie flat together, rather like an empty firefighter's hose. During arousal, however, a vagina often straightens out and puffs up even more than an erect penis – it can double in length or depth. When it is sexually aroused, the first third of the vagina becomes narrower, while the back section expands and sometimes balloons open, rather like the bottom half of an hourglass. In some women, the vagina expands before they have an orgasm and then contracts. This

Wet garbage • God • Water • A brand-new morning

Earth • Sweet ginger • Sweat • Depends • Musk • Me

Depth

No smell, I've been told • Pineapple • Chalice essence

Paloma Picasso • Earthy meat and musk • Cinnamon and cloves

Spicy musky jasmine forest, deep, deep forest • Damp moss

Roses • Yummy candy • The South Pacific • Peaches • The Woods

Ripe fruit • Heaven • Ocean • Sexy

can create a desire to experience something inside them that the rear walls can grasp during orgasm.

Received medical wisdom dictates that the first third of the vagina is more sensitive to touch, while the back two-thirds are more sensitive to pressure. There are, of course, women who would dispute this. So if you are a man reading this, check out with your female partner what her preferences are before you accept this information as set in stone.

The scent of the vagina can change according to the phase of the menstrual cycle. Around one in three women has vaginal secretions that contain certain types of scent-producing aliphatic acid chains, or organic chemical compounds. For the other 66 per cent, there is no perfume. In *The Vagina Monologues*, however, Eve Ensler asked women what they thought their vaginas smelled like and got the following answers:

Earth • Wet garbage • God • Water • A brand-new morning • Depth • Sweet ginger • Sweat • Depends • Musk • Me • No smell, I've been told • Pineapple • Chalice essence • Paloma Picasso • Earthy meat and musk • Cinnamon and cloves • Roses • Spicy musky jasmine forest, deep, deep forest • Damp moss • Yummy candy • The South Pacific • Somewhere between fish and lilacs • Peaches • The woods • Ripe fruit • Strawberry-kiwi tea • Fish • Heaven • Vinegar and water • Light, sweet liquor • Cheese • Ocean • Sexy • A sponge • The beginning

What do researchers know?

THE CERVIX

This is a fleshy little dome in the top rear part of the vagina. It is a kind of gateway that joins the uterus (womb) and the vagina. It seems incredible that the dimple in the centre of it, which is roughly the size of the top of a ballpoint pen, not only allows female fluids to descend and male fluids to travel upwards, but can also encompass the head of a baby. According to some Tantric teachers, when the area around the cervix is stimulated, it can create an effect like electricity shooting or streaming up the spine in strong, wave-like pulsations.

The cervix opens on to the uterus, the walls of which contract and expand during deeply felt orgasms. There are direct links between the nipples and the uterus and the nipples and the clitoris that allow some women to feel sexual excitement in their genitals, even though only the nipples themselves are being directly stimulated. Clever, eh?

THE OVARIES

The ovaries are two small glands, a little over 2.5 cm (1 in) long in an adult woman, which are found one on each side in the lower abdomen. Responsible for producing an egg during every menstrual cycle, they also produce the hormones that give a woman her sexual characteristics and make the cycle of fertility possible.

According to the Taoists, they are also the source of powerful energy that can revitalise the nervous system and keep you youthful and healthy. Although you won't find any woman's magazine which hails energy from the ovaries as the latest breakthrough in cosmetic wonderment, for thousands of years women followers of the Tao have practised Ovarian Breathing, where you use your mind to draw vital energy up the spine, to the head and down through the tongue, the heart, the solar plexus and finally to be stored in the navel.

It may be a while before the concept of ovary power takes over from anti-wrinkle creams, but it must be said that all the women I've met who adopt Tantric and Taoist practices look incredibly young for their years.

THE UTERUS

The uterus is about the size of a fist and lies in the lower abdomen, just above the pubic bone. A hollow muscle, the uterus can expand to nearly 100 times its original size during pregnancy. During orgasm it enlarges and contracts rhythmically.

The PC muscle

PC stands for the pubococcygeus muscle, also known as the 'love muscle' because tensing it during lovemaking tightens the grip of the vagina on the penis.

Long before 1948, when American doctor Arnold Kegel developed the pelvic floor exercises that bear his name as a treatment to strengthen the vaginal muscles and prevent incontinence, Tantric teachers were passing on to their students the importance of keeping this area of the body fit for a rewarding sex life.

The vagina is supported by the pelvic floor muscles, which are shaped like a figure-of-eight, or butterfly wings, around the vagina, urethra and anus. The largest of these muscles is the PC muscle, which connects the front of the pelvis to the lower spine. This is the muscle you rely on when you are desperate to go to the loo, but have to hold on. Both men and women use it to stop the flow of urine. Men also feel it when they bear down to squeeze out the last drops of urine. For women who have had a baby, it's the muscle you feel most acutely when you push out during childbirth.

In Tantric terms, exercising this muscle not only allows women to grip a penis more tightly, it enables them to shoot sexual energy up the spine more effectively. The rhythmic tightening and relaxation of the PC muscle happens naturally when you make love. It is also one of the main movers and shakers during orgasm. So by learning to use your PC muscle slowly and consciously, you are strengthening your ability to expand orgasmic sensations during lovemaking. Experienced practitioners of Tantra are able to reach orgasm with very little movement other than their internal muscle power.

Exercising the PC muscle

First of all, try tightening and relaxing your PC muscle in short bursts. Ideally, tighten the muscle, inhale, then relax it as you breathe out Do this, if you can, 20 times each day. The joy of this exercise is that you can do it anywhere – waiting for a bus; sitting in your car in traffic; or reading the newspaper.

When you feel comfortable with this, progress to tightening with the in-breath – retaining the breath for six seconds – and then bearing down as you exhale. This is

known as a PC Pump and, to feel a significant benefit in your lovemaking, you will need to practise it for several minutes every day. Having said that, if you manage to stick to a daily routine, Tantra teachers guarantee that within the two months it takes to strengthen and tone the PC muscle, you will notice a difference in your sex life. If you manage 30 repetitions a day, you will notice a difference in your lovemaking within a week.

Taoists are great believers in breast massage because they think that it is a powerful way of moving energy around a woman's body. Mantak Chia, the teacher and author who is credited with introducing ancient Taoist teachings to the West in the last couple of decades, gives detailed instructions on how the breasts should be massaged for optimum sexual health. These stretch over several pages, but, roughly speaking, he advocates that you should massage your breasts regularly in order to send energy throughout the hormonal system

A word of warning. Like any over-exercised muscle, the PC muscle will become sore and uncomfortable if you overdo it. So take it easy to begin with.

BREASTS

Medically speaking, breasts are mostly fatty tissue. Unlike female genitals, they are often on public display – on the beach, in low-cut tops and tight T-shirts – so it's relatively easy to see that they are all different (sometimes there can be differences even within a pair). Breasts serve two purposes: they feed babies and they are sexually arousing. Men as well as women have lots of sensitive nerve-endings in their nipples and both sexes can find being touched in this area anything from heavenly to mildly irritating.

Taoists are great believers in breast massage because they think that it is a powerful way of moving energy around a woman's body. In his book, *Healing Love Through the Tao: Cultivating Female Sexual Energy*, Mantak Chia, the teacher and author who is credited with introducing ancient Taoist teachings to the West in the last couple of decades, gives detailed instructions on how the breasts should be massaged for optimum sexual health. These stretch over several pages, but, roughly speaking, he advocates that you should massage your breasts regularly in order to send energy throughout the hormonal system. He recommends doing this sitting down, and that you inhale and rub your hands together vigorously before you begin, in order to bring energy into your palms and fingers.

Next, he says, you place your tongue on the roof of your mouth (always a vital practice when you are circulating energy around your body) and using the second, middle and fourth fingertips of both hands, move your right hand clockwise and your left hand counter-clockwise around your breasts, slowly and gently pressing against your rib-cage.

This may seem like a time-consuming exercise that does not produce immediate benefits, but if you practise it for just a short while, you will start to recognise a change in your body. I have breast implants (as a result of medical rather than cosmetic surgery) and I thought that I had virtually no feeling in my breasts as a result. Within days of practising breast massage, however, I had begun to rediscover some sensation that has increased over weeks and months. I have no idea why this should happen. This is a purely anecdotal report of the effectiveness of breast massage, but it may encourage you to give it a try.

From a general health viewpoint, should you find anything unusual in your breast, whether it is a lump, a dimple or just something that was not there before, visit your GP to have it checked out. Nine out of ten breast abnormalities are harmless, but breast cancer treatment is most effective when begun early, so it is worth investigating straightaway if you do find something amiss.

Linda, 34, marketing manager
'I have done breast massage since 1992 and it has helped lighten my periods – they only last for a couple of days now – and I feel it keeps my sexual energy moving. I was a bit cynical before trying it, and thought it might take up too much of my time, but now it's part of my daily routine and I don't even think about it any more, I just do it.'

The intimate geography of a man

Most men have a bond with their genitalia, simply because they hold their penis on average five to seven times a day when they urinate, and that's not to mention the range of games they play with it – such as the ritual involved in shaking off the last drips of pee to trouser pocket billiards. Their sexual equipment is frequently close to hand, and for many men it is a source of regular pleasure. But while they may be free of the inhibitions that some women have about their sexual organs, a man's focus on his penis can also be a distraction from the business of a truly shared experience of making love.

Society teaches us that sexual pleasure between a man and a woman depends on the man's ability to get hard and stay hard. Tantra teaches us that this is not the case:

'A real man … is signified by his passion, tenderness and consideration for his partner.'

Paul Joannides, author of *The Guide to Getting It On!*, offers my favourite definition of real manliness, which is somewhat broader than the stud who seduces dozens of women but can barely remember their names: 'A real man … is a fairly responsible person who can stand alone when the occasion demands, but who can also be warm, comforting and kind; a person who doesn't need to prove his masculinity by trying to scare or intimidate others.' To this I would add, 'The manliness of a man does not depend on the number of women he has bedded. Rather it is signified by his passion, tenderness and consideration for his partner, and his ability to make love in a spirit of giving rather than possession.'

Tantra, as you will probably have gathered by now, is not about conquering numerous partners in order to achieve sexual release.

When the British first went to India and the soldiers began to boast of their sexual prowess, the bazaar prostitutes laughed at their claims (though not, presumably to their clients' faces) and nicknamed them 'sparrows'; trivial sexual creatures whose copulation was brief and meaningless. Tantra is about creating union with a partner which brings both of you to a state of ecstasy and selfless love. And in order to achieve this, you need a sound knowledge of both your own and your partner's intimate geography.

THE PENIS

Along with the testicles (testes) and the prostate gland, this is one of the principal parts of a man's genitalia. It is made up of sponge-like tissues that surround the urethra, which is a thin tube that runs through the centre of the penis and can carry urine and semen (a handy valve shuts off the pathway to urine when a man is ready to ejaculate). The head of the penis is known as the glans. This is highly sensitive, with nearly as many nerve endings as the fingertips.

In an uncircumcised man, a rounded hood of skin called the foreskin covers the glans when the penis is relaxed. When the penis is erect, this retracts to expose the glans. Whether a man is circumcised or not makes absolutely no difference to his sexual performance, as long as the foreskin of the uncircumcised penis can move freely.

DOES SIZE MATTER?

Although the biology of the penis is relatively straightforward, millions of words have been written about it over the centuries, most of which deal with the same proposition: Does size matter? The Kama Sutra felt it necessary to address this issue, and described penises in animal terms based on size – the hare, the bull and the stallion. It matched these three types with different types of woman, but the mechanics in making this work defeat me. How can you tell the size and shape of someone's sexual organs when you are attracted to them at a party? The Taoists suggested that a man's thumb is an indication of his penis shape, and some Tantric texts claim a woman's mouth represents her vagina, but, frankly, this seems like so much whistling in the dark.

For men who feel that they would like a bigger penis, there are a number of surgical options. One involves lengthening the penis by cutting the suspensory ligament that connects the base of the penis to the pubic bone. (A penis extends back inside the body for 5–10 cm (2–4 in) and cutting the ligament releases this.) Men can also have their penis 'thickened' by having liposuction from their thighs, pubic area or hips and the fat injected into the shaft of their penis. If surgery sounds like an attractive idea, be warned. It is fairly risky, and can result in nerve damage, decreased sensation and even impotence.

More significantly, in Tantra, it is the strength of an erection that is much more important than its size. An artificially enlarged penis might be bigger, but it won't be stronger. My feeling is that the best option for a man is to meet a partner who loves him as he is and builds his sexual confidence through a good relationship. Having said this, if you are still determined to get a bigger penis, there are some exercises you can do that may create minor improvements, and if you have the time and inclination they could be worth a try.

If your penis is 'pencil-shaped' with a wider shaft, but a smaller, pointed glans, you can help the glans to get larger by squeezing the penis along its length, as though you were milking it. This will encourage the blood to flow into the glans, and over time you might notice that it becomes bigger and more mushroom-like in shape. From a woman's point of view, this is more satisfactory as a large glans

offers a thorough massage during lovemaking and helps to stimulate the walls of
the vagina and her G-spot.

To help strengthen your erection and genital muscle control, you can try
'weightlifting' with your penis (a Taoist practice). Hang a face flannel over your
erect penis, contract your muscles and see how far you can raise it. (If you want to
cheer up a miserable partner, this is practically guaranteed to raise a laugh.) As your
strength improves, you can progress from a face flannel to a small towel, and then a
bath towel, if you get really good at it.

Another exercise is equally simple. Just squeeze the shaft of your penis until it
becomes rock hard. Repeated squeezing increases the blood flow in the sponge-
like tissues of the penis and produces increasingly firm erections. Practise this for a
few minutes every day.

Although you may find exercising your penis is useful, I think it is better by far
to accept that everyone is different and, whatever your shape or size, you and your
partner will fit together happily if you both are willing to show a little
consideration, some imagination and a lot of love.

If it helps, bear in mind that there is something you can do for your partner that
will impress her far more than a surgically enlarged penis. Arouse her fully before
you enter her. If her vagina is engorged and therefore at its most sensitive, your
penis will seem bigger to her. Women generally experience most sexual sensation
in their clitoris and the first couple of inches of their vagina, which means that
even a man with a small penis can reach these most sensitive places. This suggests
to me that women are carefully designed to accept penises from men they like and
find sexy; and that if a woman is fully turned-on, penis size becomes irrelevant.

Just one more point to remember about the penis before we move on, and that
is the area known as the frenulum – an extraordinarily sensitive spot that lies just
beneath the corona, or ring of tissue that delineates the tip. Although the frenulum
has been likened to a woman's clitoris, so intense are the sensations that arise from
its stimulation, unlike the clitoris it is hard to locate. In some men, you can detect
it as a small bump, while in others there is no physical evidence at all. In this
instance, a woman can gently enquire of her partner how best to find and stimulate

this highly arousing place, remembering that, as with the clitoris, less can be more, and that a heavy-handed approach is not always welcome.

THE TESTICLES

The two testicles are enclosed within a pouch of skin, known as the scrotum, and each is linked to a spermatic cord that supplies it with blood and nerve endings, and provides a duct (the vas deferens) along which sperm passes after it has been produced by the testicle. The testicles also produce testosterone, the male sex hormone. As I am sure you are well aware, when the penis becomes aroused (or, rather, the brain of the owner of the penis becomes aroused) it swells up and becomes erect. (The testicles also swell during sexual arousal, and pull up tight against the body.)

Rhythmic contractions of the prostate gland (see below), seminal vesicles (a small pair of sac-like glands above the prostate which produce most of the fluid that becomes semen) and the vas deferens pump semen into the base of the urethra. When ejaculation occurs, the semen is forced along the urethra and out of the tip of the penis by another series of contractions, primarily coming from the urethra itself and the muscles at the base and along the shaft of the penis.

One of the main tenets of Tantra is the ability of the man to control his ejaculation, thus ending disappointment for one or both partners when sex is brought to an unwanted conclusion. This ability to separate ejaculation and orgasm – experiencing an orgasm without inevitably ejaculating at the same time – is dealt with in greater detail in Chapter Four. But in order to understand the technicalities behind this, it's important to be aware of a man's physical and mental wiring. This is where the prostate comes in.

THE PROSTATE GLAND

The prostate plays a critical role in male sexuality. It is a chestnut-shaped gland that surrounds the urethra near the point at which it leaves the bladder. (One of the early warning signs of prostate problems is the need to urinate frequently, accompanied by poor flow, which is often due to enlargement of the prostate. If

WITH SOME

PRACTICE, AND A

DEGREE OF

DETERMINATION,

YOU WILL BE

ABLE TO

EXPERIENCE AN

ORGASM

WITHOUT

EJACULATION

AND BE ON THE

PATHWAY TO

ACHIEVING

MULTIPLE

ORGASMS

you need to urinate frequently, have difficulty starting or stopping or you notice blood in your urine, make sure you consult your GP.) During sexual arousal, the prostate expands and secretes a clear fluid that is an important ingredient of semen (it makes about one-third of ejaculate and is responsible for its whitish colour). Its contractions during ejaculation are partly responsible for the pleasurable feelings associated with the male orgasm.

The prostate, like the G-spot for women, is highly sensitive to sexual stimulation. Like the G-spot, it becomes increasingly sensitive to stimulation as a man becomes aroused and approaches orgasm. This is why a prostate check-up with your doctor is about as different from prostate stimulation in bed with your lover as a thorn from a rose.

You can reach the prostate from inside and outside the body. There are women who proudly boast they can massage a man's prostate from inside his anus and thus reduce him to a heap of gibbering pleasure. There are also women for whom the idea of putting their fingers anywhere near their partner's anus (even in a latex glove) is an instant turn-off. As Tantra is about exploration of each other's bodies with respect, never cajole or force a partner to do anything that he or she is not comfortable with.

It is possible to ejaculate through prostatic stimulation alone, although in this instance the fluid generally flows out rather than gushes out in spurts. Some men report that prostate orgasms are very different, physically and emotionally, from orgasms linked to the penis. The level of stimulation is certainly very deep and intense.

If the idea of stimulating the prostate from inside the body does not appeal, all is not lost. It can be reached through the perineum (a stretch of skin between the testicles and the anus), at the spot encouragingly known by Taoists as the Million Dollar Point (MDP). This was originally called the Million-Gold Piece Point in Ancient China because that is supposedly what it then cost to have a Taoist master teach you its exact location. (Clearly, the Taoists had one eye on heaven and the other on market values.)

The MDP is an area that lies on the perineum, just in front of the anus. Known by Taoists as The Gate of Life and Death, it is not only highly sensitive to stimulation, but it also plays a vital role in stopping ejaculation. If you press on your MDP with the index and middle fingers of one hand, you can prevent semen leaving your prostate and entering the urethra for ejaculation, effectively stopping the ejaculatory response, without affecting your ability to experience an orgasm (see Chapter Four).

The PC muscle

Like women, men have a group of muscles that run from the pubic bone ('pubo') in the front of their body to the tailbone or coccyx ('coccygeus') in the back. Known as the pubococcygeus, or PC muscle, they form the basis of your sexual health and are essential for multiple orgasms (in both sexes). It is vital to exercise these muscles, as if they are under-used, they become wasted and weak, in exactly the same way as under-exercised muscles in the rest of your body. The penis, for example, actually withdraws into the body if it is not used regularly, as older men who are not sexually active will testify.

Control of the PC muscle is critical for men who want to practise Tantric sex, as this is the muscle that enables you to separate orgasmic response from ejaculation. When you are fairly experienced at this, you will notice that by contracting your PC muscle when you are at the threshold of an orgasm you will be able to delay ejaculation. With some practice, and a degree of determination, you will be able to experience an orgasm without ejaculation and be on the pathway to achieving multiple orgasms. (Contracting the PC muscle is also good for your prostate as the contractions massage and stimulate the gland at the same time.)

Exercising the PC muscle

Broadly speaking, men can exercise their PC muscle in the same way as women. Men, however, are most aware of their PC muscle when they are trying to push out the last few drops of urine. The PC muscle is also what allows animals to wag their tails. Interestingly enough, the word penis means 'tail' in Latin, so exercising

Recently, researchers have found that some men become irritable or depressed when their testosterone level is raised. They have also discovered that men have mood shifts that are every bit as strong as women's, if not more so. So the myth that only women are slaves to their hormones, is just that – a myth

your PC muscle teaches you to 'wag your tail' in order to strengthen your erections, intensify your orgasms and separate your orgasms from ejaculation.

Because the bladder and the prostate are so close, you should urinate before self-pleasuring or lovemaking whenever your bladder feels full. A full bladder will make you feel like you need to ejaculate and can actually make it more difficult for your to stop yourself from ejaculating, if that is what you want to do.

If you have a strong PC muscle, you should be able to stop the flow of urine midstream and then start it again. If you find this difficult, the chances are your PC muscle is weak and could do with some exercise. Stopping the flow of urine may sting at first. This is normal and should stop within a couple of weeks, although if it doesn't, you might have an infection. If this is the case, visit your GP and wait until it has cleared up before you continue.

In his book, *The Multi-Orgasmic Man*, Mantak Chia recommends that men stand on their toes and the balls of their feet; inhale deeply; then exhale slowly, forcefully pushing out the urine while pulling up in their perineum and clenching their teeth. Then they should inhale and contract the PC muscle to stop the flow of urine midstream, exhale and start urinating again. This should be repeated three to six times, or until they have finished urinating.

Admittedly, this sounds like awfully hard work. If you don't feel up to it, or you are understandably concerned that it will earn you some strange looks in the Gents', simply stop and start urinating as many times as you can. Standing on your toes and clenching your teeth just intensifies the exercise.

Similarly, the PC pull-ups Mantak Chia recommends include squeezing the muscles around the eyes and mouth at the same time as you tense the muscles around your anus and perineum. Again, this could be tricky in company. However, you can inhale and tense your PC muscle, exhale and release it as many times as you can while picking up your email or sitting in a dull meeting. No one will know. The main objective is to do this exercise two or three times a day; but don't push yourself too hard. Muscles can get sore and the important thing is to be consistent rather than to overload your body erratically.

MALE HORMONES

Testosterone is the primary hormone responsible for sperm production and a man's sex drive. Testosterone levels may drop slightly with age, in the same way as other bodily functions tend to slow down too. But although you may find it takes longer to achieve an erection in your seventies compared to the time it took in your twenties, you still maintain the ability to give and receive sexual pleasure. Although a certain level of testosterone is necessary for this, it isn't a very high amount. Increasing the amount artificially will not give a man a stronger sex drive. The only time when added hormones will increase his libido is when his testosterone level is below the minimum to begin with.

Recently, researchers have found that some men become irritable or depressed when their testosterone level is raised. They have also discovered that men have mood shifts that are every bit as strong as women's, if not more so. So the myth that only women are slaves to their hormones, is just that – a myth.

3

WOMEN
AND TANTRA

Despite the claims on the front of women's magazines that we are all multi-orgasmic now and that sex has never been better, there are still lots of women who feel disappointed or let down by sex. (And even if you enjoy a good sex life, isn't there is always scope for improvement?)

The good news for women is that Tantra places the satisfaction of the woman as either equal to or above that of the man (depending on which version of it you examine). And the even better news for some of us is that female powerful sexuality does not stem from a requirement to look or behave a certain way. You don't have to be a leggy blonde, resemble a movie star or be under 40 to radiate a potent sexual energy that will draw men to you.

In Tantra, women's sexuality is acknowledged as the fuel that drives the couple's sexual experience. This isn't to say that men are in any way inferior to women, but Tantra is a world away from the average two minutes of lovemaking that, according to one US survey, is experienced by most couples. (Or the 'wham, bam, thank you mam' approach, which leaves so many women inclined to give up on sex altogether.)

Modern sexual statistics can make depressing reading. In a 2001 survey commissioned by Britain's *Top Santé* magazine, out of 3000 women, with an average age of 38, 95 per cent said the appearance of their bodies depressed them; nearly two-thirds thought they would have better sex if they had an ideal body, and 42 per cent preferred to undress with the lights off. Editor Juliet Kellow commented: 'For almost 40 years, being attractive has been equated with being thin. But women's desire for body perfection is no longer just a weight issue – the majority of the normal-sized and underweight women answering our survey were still unhappy with their bodies. The problem is, we live in an age of perfection which leaves most women feeling imperfect.'

JO, 35, TV DIRECTOR

'For most of my adult life I've hated my stomach and thighs. People joke about the woman who constantly asks "Does my bum look big in this?" but I actually think that more times than I care to admit.'

FOOD AS PUNISHMENT

Since the 1960s, millions of naturally curvy women have struggled to conform to a boyish figure first popularised by a stick-thin Twiggy. Until 1960, a typical model was curvy, not skinny, and her shape was roughly in line with that of the rest of the female population – she weighed only about 8 per cent less that the average woman. Today's supermodels weigh at least 25 per cent less than the average woman, and the influence they exert on other women is far from healthy.

How do we get back to that place where a woman felt like a goddess, no matter what her shape or size? What can women do to be joyfully in touch with their bodies; to be bold or soft; creative or nurturing? And how can you learn to be downright sexy, even if you think you've got thighs the size of a sumo wrestler?

Millions of women are on weight-loss diets (health experts estimate it's one out of every two at any given time). Or they are guilty about not dieting, and as a result feel bad about virtually everything they eat. For many women food has become a form of punishment or guilt, rather than a source of joy.

Most women I have talked to about Tantra have looked at me as though I'm mad when I say that in Tantra a woman needs to love her body, and to believe that she deserves a man who will treat her body with adoration and respect. Too many women, it seems, feel they somehow have to be thin to qualify as being sexually desirable, and that their bodies let them down. 'What – love these thighs/hips/breasts?' is their cry. 'I don't think so.'

And while we're freefalling down the escalator of sexual despair (don't worry – there is a way back up), let us remember that in some respects the sexual liberation that the 1960s brought us has turned out to be a mixed blessing. Women may be more sexually active, but a greater quantity of lovers doesn't necessarily imply a corresponding increase in the quality of the lovemaking. How many women today feel revered and honoured as goddesses by their partners? Not many. The idea is enough to make most women giggle in disbelief.

Tantra, on the other hand, encourages men to look beyond outward appearances and to treat women with awe and reverence. And we are not talking about men honouring the idealised, simpering, weak kind of woman that some men find it easy to put on a pedestal. Tantric texts, according to the scholar Miranda Shaw in her book *Passionate Enlightenment*, portray bold, outspoken, independent women. 'Tantric practices describe how women should be respected, served and ritually worshipped,' says Shaw. 'Tantric theory advances an ideal of cooperative, mutually liberating relationships between men and women.'

So if men and women practised a Tantric ideal thousands of years ago, where did it all go wrong? And how do we get back to that place where a woman felt like a goddess, no matter what her shape or size? What can women do to be joyfully in touch with their bodies; to be bold or soft; creative or nurturing? And how can you learn to be downright sexy, even if you think you've got thighs the size of a sumo wrestler?

Here are my thoughts.

The Hammer of Witches ...

Female sexuality has rarely been fêted and wholeheartedly approved of by men. Women can be celebrated as mothers or sex queens, but not both. It is the Madonna/whore syndrome that divides women into the categories of 'good' or 'bad'.

Tantra encourages men to look

beyond outward appearances

and to treat women

with awe and

reverence

Probably the most significant man in history to ignore any such division was Jesus, who treated his mother Mary and his friend, the supposed prostitute, Mary Magdalene, with even-handed respect. According to the Rev. Mary Robins of St James' Church, Piccadilly:

'Jesus taught and healed women, which we take for granted these days, but in those days it was absolutely culture-shattering. Not only was a woman's place in the home, she was regarded as the property of a man; either her husband, father, uncle or son, and she was not considered to be worth educating.

The early church fathers did not share his attitude. They lived as hermits in the desert. A lot of their writings are about how awful women are. I think they were projecting onto women their own fears about bodies and struggles with celibacy. Because the Christian religion has developed through the words and minds and experiences of these men, these have been expressed by the Church, but they are not the total truth of humanity.'

The early Christian church set a pattern of repression against female sexuality that existed for centuries. In 1484, Pope Innocent VIII became concerned about an outbreak of witchcraft that was said to have taken place in Northern Germany. He appointed two Dominican monks, Heinrich Kramer and James Sprenger – both members of the Inquisition – to investigate and stamp it out. The two men wrote the *Malleus Maleficarum* (The Hammer of Witches), first published around 1486 and regularly reprinted until 1669. These two warped individuals – not the kind of single guys you'd want to invite to your barbecue – were hugely influential. Their rants against women were swallowed wholesale by an ignorant populace.

'All witchcraft comes from carnal lust, which is in women insatiable,' they declared. 'But the natural reason [why a woman is intellectually inferior] is that she is more carnal than a man, as is clear from her many carnal abominations. And it should be noted that there was a defect in the formation of the first woman, since she was formed from a bent rib, that is rib of the breast, which is bent as it were in a contrary direction to a man. And since through this defect she is an imperfect animal, she always deceives.'

According to *The Woman's Encyclopaedia of Myths and Secrets*, it was at a witch's trial in 1593 that the investigating lawyer (a married man) discovered a clitoris for the first time. He identified it as a devil's teat, sure proof of the witch's guilt. It was

'a little lump of flesh, in manner sticking out as if it has been a teat, to the length of half an inch,' which the gaoler, 'perceiving at the first sight thereof, meant not to disclose, because it was adjoining to so secret a place which was not decent to be seen. Yet in the end, not willing to conceal so strange a matter, he showed it to various bystanders. The bystanders had never seen anything like it. The witch was convicted.'

Some men, trapped in the fear and ignorance of their forefathers, have sought to control female sexuality over the centuries and mould it to their will. In the 1800s girls who learned to develop orgasmic capacity by masturbation were regarded as medical cases. Often they were 'treated' or 'corrected' by amputation of the clitoris, by the creation of 'miniature chastity belts', which involved sewing the vaginal lips together to put the clitoris out of reach, or even surgical removal of the ovaries. In the United States, the last recorded clitoridectomy for curing masturbation was performed in 1948 – on a five-year-old girl. In the 21st century, some cultures are still imposing female circumcision on their young girls with horrendous consequences for their sexual health and life-threatening implications when they give birth.

So perhaps it's small wonder that most women have inherited mixed feelings about their sexuality from their mothers. Western women may no longer be physically subjugated to men, but just as they have managed to shake off past prejudice and repression, they have jumped into the fire of self-imposed tyranny about their body shape and appearance which restricts joy and delight in their sexuality as surely as if they were physically locked up in chastity belts by jealous lords and masters.

Some

app

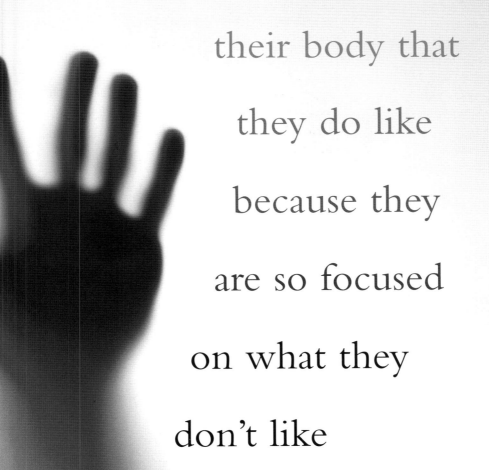

mes, women don't even

eciate that there are parts of

their body that

they do like

because they

are so focused

on what they

don't like

Instead of submitting to this, consider how you can best develop your confidence as a powerful sexual being, for if you are a woman, that is your birthright, and the sooner you claim it, the richer your life will be.

HOW TO FEEL COMFORTABLE WITH YOURSELF

Every woman is unique, and can feel good in different ways. The following suggestions might help. Choose what you feel most comfortable with and try those first. These are pointers that have helped other women to move on from negative images and feelings about themselves and these may be useful to you too.

First things first. You don't have to feel fantastic about your body before you begin to practise Tantra. And there is every chance that making a decision to practise some Tantric techniques will help you start to feel more confident anyway. Eventually, feeling good about yourself will enable you get the most out of Tantra, and the better you feel about yourself, the more fully you will be able to give to your partner. This is because you will be giving from a place of confidence, equality and independence, rather than the needy philosophy of 'I'll give to you only because I need you to give something to me in return.'

THE TANTRIC LOVE YOURSELF DIET

Tantra teacher Leora experienced this positive impact of Tantra for herself:

'When I started doing Tantra I was two stone heavier than I am now, and I had quite a big tummy. I didn't like my tummy and I saw it as a sign that I was out of control and that this was a bad thing. So it wasn't just that I didn't like the aesthetics, but I thought that somehow I was bad being the weight that I was, and that was symbolized by my tummy. So first of all I changed my relationship with my tummy. I saw it as more feminine and rounded. As I came to like it more, it no longer signified something bad and horrible but signified something pleasant. The same situation was there, but my feelings around it had changed.

I was trying to lose weight desperately before then, because I didn't like how I was, and I kept putting it back on. But then, as I started to like my body, the weight loss happened completely spontaneously. As I started to love myself more, I had more energy and I imagine the weight loss came through cycling, doing more exercise and being more energetic. I honestly don't recall doing anything different to lose that weight, apart from being more physically active.

I stopped trying to lose weight because I was happier with how I was and, ironically, that meant I stopped gaining weight. I much prefer being the weight I am now. I feel lighter and happier, but I did get to the stage where I was happy being chubby. My husband met me when I was heavier and he is disappointed that I have lost weight!

I don't know if I can promote this as "The Tantric Love Yourself" diet! But I can certainly promote it as a way of being happier and more at home in your body.'

Leading Tantra workshops, Leora encounters a stream of women who would like to feel better about their bodies:

'One of the things that constantly strikes me and other women who participate in the groups is that although we have a cultural model of beauty which tends to be under 20, tall and slim, with well endowed breasts, even people who look pretty close to that model often don't love themselves. In fact, sometimes women who are traditionally beautiful have a hard time feeling loved because they think that men like them simply for their bodies. They find it harder to know that they are loved for who they are.

Generally speaking it is on a scale, but most women will have some barriers to feeling fully great in themselves. Some people are pretty happy with themselves, but I've never met a woman who couldn't love herself a little bit more.

We do an exercise in Tantra which is a very strong way of helping us first of all to elicit our negative beliefs about ourselves. Often what happens is that we have our inner critics in our heads that are so familiar that they are just like background noise, and when we focus on our bodies, they have their particular liturgy – something along the lines of "Your thighs are too fat; your breasts aren't big enough; you should exercise more" – and when we can start to actually speak those words in connection with our bodies, and hear our negative beliefs out loud, women are quite shocked at how powerful these thoughts are.

CATHY, 51,
PUBLIC
RELATIONS MANAGER

'When I did this woman-only exercise on a Tantra holiday, I found it very intimidating, because you always assume that other women are going to be very judgemental about you. But it was enlightening. I was taken aback by how nice they were! And it made me realize that other people don't see you the way that you see yourself. It dawned on me that the way people act is very much to do with them and not me. Other people don't see things through my eyes, so I shouldn't waste time worrying about what they notice about me. The chances are what they notice won't be what I worry about. Appreciating this has given me more confidence in myself. And I feel much calmer as a result.'

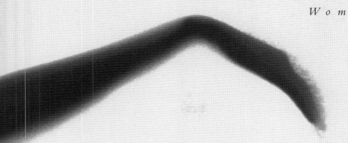

When they go unrecognised, when we can't speak them out loud, it is as if we become identified with those beliefs and they are entirely part of us. Speaking our negative beliefs gives us a sense of separation from them and that is vitally important.

My exercise with women involves groups of threes. Each woman takes it in turn to stand in front of the other two, and even that moment of standing in front of two people to be seen is very powerful. Then she consciously undresses, and as she removes each item of clothing, she sets the intention of letting go of some of the layers of shame and self-criticism that prevent them from really loving themselves. When she has taken off as many clothes as she feels comfortable with, she will either be naked or scantily dressed in front of the group. Many women say they are used to being naked around other women in swimming baths or the gym, but actually being looked at is different.

What is also different in the exercise is that when we have a negative self-image, we imagine that we are being scrutinised with a critical eye and what happens in a workshop environment is that the other women will be looking not to criticise but to appreciate the woman as she is. And if she is able to be present mentally as well as physically, she will see this. The healing comes from allowing our negative beliefs from the past to be present, while also discovering a new reality.

Sometimes that transformation is not instantaneous, but over time, as women allow those negative thoughts to become more separated, so they don't identify totally with those negative thoughts any more, there is some space to learn to receive something new.

The next step in the exercise is for the woman to describe the parts of her body that she does not like and to show them to the other two women, and they don't comment, they just accept that this is how the woman who is speaking feels about her body. Then she speaks about the parts of her body she does like. Sometimes, women don't even appreciate that there are parts of their body that they do like because they are so focused on what they don't like. So they start to get more of a balanced view of themselves. It also gives women a chance to think about what they don't like and the function or significance that has in their lives.

The other women then give feedback on what touches them about the woman in front of them, and that gives her a chance to look at herself in a positive new way. When you see someone else standing up, usually you can see the beauty in her body straightaway, whatever shape or size it is. You notice yourself gasping with surprise when you hear someone with beautiful breasts say they don't like their breasts. You notice how your reality and theirs are different, and how theirs is almost inevitably harsher than yours. So by default, you can see that your own judgements about your body are likely to be much tougher than those that other people might make.

The final stage of the exercise is to receive some nourishing contact from the other women in the form of gentle touch or a light massage.

One of the huge benefits of going to a workshop is that you are with other people. Usually, we have acquired our negative beliefs about ourselves and our bodies through other people and, although you can heal on your own, I think it is more beneficial to find some way of doing it with others. Even if it's just something that you decide to do with a group of close women friends, having that outside female support is so helpful.'

CATHY, 51, PUBLIC RELATIONS MANAGER
'When I did this woman-only exercise on a Tantra holiday, I found it very intimidating, because you always assume that other women are going to be very judgemental about you. But it was enlightening. I was taken aback by how nice they were! And it made me realize that other people don't see you the way that you see yourself. It dawned on me that the way people act is very much to do with them and not me. Other people don't see things through my eyes, so I shouldn't waste time worrying about what they notice about me. The chances are what they notice won't be what I worry about. Appreciating this has given me more confidence in myself. And I feel much calmer as a result.'

If you don't like the idea of trying an exercise like this with other women, but you would still like to feel happier with your body, there are plenty of other steps you can take to set you on the road to feeling good about yourself.

BE SENSUAL WITH YOUR BODY

When you are having a bath or shower, be conscious of touching your body as you wash yourself rather than slipping into automatic mode and thinking about work, your children or the coat you have to collect from the cleaners. Buy a delicious-smelling body lotion and as you rub it into your body, try to have a sense of doing this with love and with the idea that you are taking care of yourself. 'Being sensual with one's body is very powerful,' says Leora. 'Just being conscious of simple pleasure allows you to get more in touch with your body.'

As an exercise this is not difficult and it's not even time-consuming. Leora also recommends standing in front of a mirror and noticing how you feel when you are naked. Look into your own eyes and observe your reaction to doing this. It might not feel comfortable at first, but the more you do it, the sooner you will start to notice changes in the way you feel about your body. 'Anything that helps you live in the present, rather than worrying about the past or the future is helpful too,' she says. 'Dancing, meditation or Tai Chi are all good. Working with your chakras helps too, because that transforms you from the inside.'

CHANGE YOUR POSTURE

According to Leora, even consciously changing your posture can make a big difference to how you feel about yourself. 'I recently worked with a woman who was very hunched,' she says. 'She said she felt as though she needed to protect her chest and she felt as though she did this because people somehow wanted to invade her boundaries. So we practised looking at how that felt and how it felt by way of contrast when she stood upright. She realised that she felt much more powerful when she was upright and more like a sexy woman and that was quite a dramatic change for her.'

Before you can consider how to improve your emotional relationship with your body, you need to think carefully about you current attitude towards it. According to Priyatama, a teacher who runs courses on Healing for Intimacy with the US-based Human Awareness Institute, lots of women are so busy with their day-to-day lives that they live only in their heads.

'Men tend to be more grounded and present in their bodies,' she explains. 'Women are rushing around with work, taking care of children and their families and they tend not to take the time to be really present and aware of their own bodies.

Whatever your shape and size, you need to begin to take care of your body and to nourish it with good quality food. Only put good things into it – and that includes your choice of male organs! Be in contact with your body. I stroke my body a lot. I do dry skin brushing, which makes my body feel alive and tingly and then I use essential oils. When I stroke my body in a sensual way, I might end up getting sexual pleasure from it, but that is not my main aim. I treat my body in the way that I would like someone else to treat it.'

One helpful biological fact to remember is that women's bodies are designed to have gently rounded tummies. The phenomenon of the flat female stomach is a recent one and, according to Tantric practice, it isn't advisable. Women store powerful female energy in their bellies and by trying to flatten them to look like men they are losing out on an integral part of their femininity. If you are a woman who has spent hours in the gym and you are delighted with your flat stomach, you don't have to abandon your sit-ups straightaway. If your stomach makes you feel good, stick with it. But if you are a woman who hates her rounded tummy, try thinking of it as a symbol of your feminine power instead of something to feel bad about. You may be surprised at how soon you start to like it more.

An agenda for a
would-be sex goddess ...

If you feel unhappy with your looks, here is an agenda for a would-be sex goddess. It is about making the most of yourself, staying as healthy as you can, and then finding something more interesting to do.

- Get a good haircut and the kind of make-over on offer from any department store beauty counter. If it gives you a boost, buy the make-up they suggest and use it.

- Abandon the idea of 'going on a diet'; dieting makes most women miserable and is the antithesis of the kind of experience you need to feel good about yourself. The entire multi-million pound dieting industry can be summed up in four words 'Eat less, exercise more'. So eat fruit instead of sugary snacks, stick to three regular meals a day and walk rather than take the car if you are allergic to other forms of exercise. Within days you will start to feel good. Within weeks you will feel better about your body.

- If you are looking for a role model, choose a woman who's achieved something you admire through her courage, intelligence or determination. Most women who've found fame purely because of their looks tend to be unhappy, neurotic individuals who deserve your sympathy, rather than your admiration. Knowing your appeal has a limited shelf-life doesn't do much for anyone's self-esteem.

'My ideas about women's sexuality have definitely changed. I can see that sensuality and sexual potency are present in women, whether they are voluptuously curvy, or elegantly slender. I definitely love and appreciate my body more than I did before and I feel sexually powerful. Sometimes the old patterns of worry about my body come up, but it just doesn't bother me so much now.'

AGEING — ONE OF OUR GREATEST FEARS

In the West, one of our biggest fears is the process of growing older. Other societies have different attitudes to ageing. In traditional Aboriginal culture, older women are seen as extremely sexually attractive and will often have sexual partners who are much younger. Most Western women, though, worry that their bodies will fall apart and no one will fancy them any more. There are two responses to this. The first is that if you take reasonable care of your body, eat well, take a decent amount of exercise and don't smoke, you should stay fit and healthy for many decades. (The age of your suitors may rise, but then, you will be older too …)

The other response is to accept that ageing is normal and that it brings its own rewards. Which sane woman would give up her children and the joy they have brought her in return for a flat stomach and no stretch marks? As Dr Victoria Lee points out in her book, *Soulful Sex*:

[We have been] taught to strive for youth and beauty and 'style' as the alleged keys to happiness. In this milieu, the only possible view of ageing is that it is synonymous with loss.

Lovemaking, according to these same values, is best enjoyed when you are physically beautiful. The more you look like a model or a bodybuilder, the better your orgasms will be and the more your partner will love you.

The truth is quite different. The truth is that sex is best enjoyed when we are spiritually and psychologically developed enough to love ourselves — body, mind and spirit. This must be our first aim. Second, we may grow more and more willing to love our partners fully. The more we can love and accept ourselves and our partners, the greater our joy in lovemaking.

At sixty, we may hope to be better able to love than at thirty; at seventy, we can aspire to love better than at sixty, and so on, as long as we are given the gift of life. It's never to late to finally gain self-acceptance and to learn to love well.

An extract from the poem 'Canzone For A Young Girl' by William Anderson, reflects this idea perfectly:

Suppose
That from the red rose head you shook
The rainbeads on each petal's curl
And in the lifeline of your palm you cupped
The drops that are all soul of rose.
You touch them with your tongue. Scent throws
From brain to limbs prophetic power.
The petals can break off and die
And you'll not mind for you know why
That what is dead is not the flower –
Just as a woman smiles and knows
That time which ruins beauty, health,
May not attack her ground of self.

If you are in touch with your 'ground of self' as a woman, if you are at ease in your own skin, no matter what your body shape, growing old will not fill you with terror. It is simply another destination on your life's journey. (An added bonus is that you are less likely to feel under pressure in some kind of imagined competition with the rest of the women in the world.)

One other point to bear in mind is that it is natural for people to admire beauty in all its forms. So if your partner looks at a younger woman, that is all they are doing – looking. Could you, as a woman, put your hand on your heart and say that your eyes have never followed a handsome young man as he's walked by? Watching

A Tantric relationship is based on so much more than physical appearance or the number of birthdays you've had. In a Tantric partnership, you honour the inner self of the other person your partner idly look at someone else is not a cue to get neurotic and anxious that your partner will leave you for the object of his glance.

One of the reasons why men are more frequently accused by their partners of ogling other women is that their peripheral vision is not as good as a woman's. In their book, *Why Men Don't Listen and Women Can't Read Maps* – an entertaining romp through recent scientific research into the brain differences between men and women – authors Allan and Barbara Pease point out that a woman's brain software allows her to receive an arc of at least 45 degrees clear vision to each side of her head and above and below her nose. Many women's peripheral vision is effective up to almost 180 degrees.

They argue that as hunters, men needed vision that would allow them to zoom in and pursue targets in the distance. As a result they evolved with almost blinkered vision so that they would not be distracted from their prey. Women, on the other hand, needed eyes to allow a wide arc of vision so that they could monitor any predators sneaking up on their nests. A woman's wider peripheral vision means that she rarely gets caught staring at other men, even though sex researchers report that women look at men's bodies as much as, and sometimes more than, men look at women's.

And anyway a Tantric relationship is based on so much more than physical appearance or the number of birthdays you've had. In a Tantric partnership, you honour the inner self of the other person. A relationship built purely on physical attraction, with no connection on a mental or spiritual level, is bound to disintegrate sooner rather than later.

THE GOOD NEWS

One heartening piece of social research suggested that men find their partners increasingly attractive as they grow older, which destroys the myth that most men would eagerly drop a 40-year-old wife for a 20-year-old if they had half a chance. (Some men do, of course. This tends to come from a desperation to overlook their own ageing process. It may sound brutal, but trying to establish a truly Tantric relationship with a man haunted by mid-life demons is probably doomed to failure.)

Women who judge themselves against celebrities and models and feel depressed are being conned into feeling inadequate by marketing and media hype that isn't based on anything remotely like real life. As a journalist, I have sat in on photographic sessions and seen the hours of work it takes an entire team of makeup artists, stylists and hairdressers to make naturally beautiful models and actresses look good for the camera. It's inevitable that any ordinary woman who tries to compete with them is bound to feel less attractive. Give up comparing yourself with women on TV or pictured in magazines. A lot of them have distorted body images and unhealthy relationships with food. Bulimia and anorexia, two frighteningly self-destructive illnesses, are common among women who earn money from their looks.

For the foreseeable future, we are probably not going to get away from seeing skinny women modelling clothes. Designers use them because they are the easiest shape to dress in absolutely anything, but that does not mean that if you are a size 16 or over there aren't plenty of things in which you can look stunning too.

If you talk to men about what they find attractive in a woman, they will often point out that the reason they are drawn to the women who appear on advertising images is that these women give off messages that they are open to and interested in sex. These images are, of course, carefully manipulated and ultimately fake. But the principle holds true for real people. Sex researchers have noted that there is a direct correlation between someone's personal confidence in their sexuality and their ability to enjoy sex.

RACHEL, 34, LECTURER

'Since I took up Tantra I have become much more confident in my own body. In the past I would never allow myself to wear a low-cut top, I almost felt that I had to keep myself hidden away. But now I accept myself and I allow myself to be sexy if I want to; it is such a feeling of liberation.'

Women who feel sexy may differ dramatically in looks, but they share an attitude – they know that whatever the world may make of their outward appearance, they are comfortable in their own skins and they know they are desirable.

LINDA, 34, MARKETING MANAGER

'I have seen women who practise Tantric and Taoist techniques and they are a million miles away from the Hollywood stereotype of what is sexy, but they radiate sex appeal. These women are in their fifties and sixties. I met one woman who was 58 and she was one of the sexiest people I have ever seen; she had such a powerful sexual confidence. It made someone like Pamela Anderson look so superficial. Pamela Anderson may be quite a nice person, but feeling that you ought to look like her takes away women's power. Tantra gives it back.'

LOOSENING THOSE FETTERS

Unfastening psychological fetters may take time, but Tantra gives you the tools to start, even though it may be a while before you feel negative ways of thinking about yourself begin to lose their hold on you.

In Tantra, since your relationship is built on love and respect for one another, a partner who genuinely loves you will be pretty much blind to any defects you may perceive about your body. Ninety-nine per cent of men rate a sense of humour more highly than a cellulite-free body. Men make love to a whole woman, not just a pair of thighs. For a Tantric relationship to be successful, it is important that you believe that your inner self and the inner self of your partner deserves to be honoured.

If you have serious doubts about this, you may be in the wrong relationship. Practising Tantra with someone puts your partnership under a spotlight. If the relationship has cracks in it they may be magnified. It is up to every woman and man to be confident in their positive feelings for their partner before exploring Tantra together. Tantra may be a healing balm for an injured relationship, but it is not a miracle cure.

NATALIE, 28, DESIGNER

'It may sound like an unpopular point of view, but I think that a lot of women are compliant in their own sexual misery. I stayed in bad relationships because I didn't have the courage to leave and because I didn't want to be on my own. I used to blame my lovers for being crap. But in those days my attitude was that his orgasm mattered far more than mine;

he would have to come first and if he could be bothered, then there might be a bit of time for me at the end, in which case there was usually too much pressure and I couldn't do it anyway. That was my whole attitude to sex.

Now I have explored my sexuality a lot more and I know that it takes two people to have a bad sex life. My views began to change when I got the courage to live on my own and I realised that being on your own is a lot better than being in a bad relationship. I don't blame those men in my past now, and I'm able to admit that a lot of my unhappiness had to do with me, and my behaviour. Also, I know that it takes two people to have a good relationship that encompasses good sex too.'

How to ask for what you want

When most women begin a physical relationship with someone new, they have a desire to please their partner, but few have the ability to ask easily for pleasure themselves. In the West, most of the role models for sex come from porn films or Hollywood, both of which tend to offer a fairly one-dimensional view of men as the active instigators of the sexual act and women as the passive and enthusiastic receivers.

As a result, most modern men believe it is their job to 'give' their partner an orgasm, preferably before achieving one themselves, and if the woman doesn't reach orgasm they may feel that in some way they have failed as men. As a result, millions of women have learnt to fake orgasms over the years, simply so that their partners, whom they care about, don't end up feeling failures in bed.

There are problems with this rather limited approach to sex. Firstly, it sets the goal of orgasm as a target for both partners. This puts pressure on both parties, especially on men, who can think they are solely responsible for ensuring that everyone has a great time sexually. Failure to perform in this respect can hit a man harder than many women think, so it is never a good idea for a woman to mock a man who is trying to give her a good time, even if he's as far away from her clitoris as Minnesota.

A Tantric relationship is one of equals, where communication flows easily between you. And sex is not restricted to a sprint towards joint orgasm. You have

If you really don't
know where to
begin, bear in
mind that the
line of a woman's
spine, from the
back of her neck
to the cleft
between her
buttocks is well
supplied
with nerve
endings and
usually
craves
attention

the option to explore each other's bodies as you might a foreign country, to get to know each other's terrain and to find favourite and familiar places.

NATALIE, 28, DESIGNER

'With my ex-boyfriend, when we had sex there was very little foreplay, and if there was it was solely with the intention of us both having an orgasm so we could finish and go to sleep. I used to describe our sex life as galloping towards orgasm as fast as possible.

Now with my new partner, who has practised Tantra for several years, when I am just on my way to orgasm I think 'This is fantastic, it is lovely right where I am'. I enjoy the journey rather than constantly focus on the destination. And if you enjoy the journey, the destination ends up being ten times as good; it's a double whammy.

Western sex is so tied up with orgasm, primarily male orgasm, that often women have to run along beside, trying to keep up. Making love in a Tantric way is an entirely different experience. Now I have orgasms which are so much more than the typical kind of flutter. They go on an awful lot longer and they might plateau and then go up a bit more. It breaks your usual definition of what an orgasm is meant to be.

Before I became interested in a more spiritual approach to sex, I probably would never have said that my sex life needed much attention, but I didn't feel very sexual as a woman. But with my present partner, my sexual energy has got much higher and much more creative. I feel that my sexuality is something that I can continue to explore.'

Communicating your needs to your partner as equals sounds sensible, but some women find this hard to do without worrying that they will appear aggressive or demanding. Giving feedback to your partner and asking for what you want while you are making love is best done through soft noises of encouragement ('Mmm, that's nice, more please') and gently placing your partner's hands where you would like them, rather than delivering detailed instructions in a sergeant-major style bark.

If you want to try something dramatically new, it's best to discuss it with your partner before you disappear into the bedroom or wherever you choose to make love together. This will give them the chance to say No if they want to, or simply talk it through beforehand.

If you are nervous about asking for what you would like in bed, follow these simple guidelines:

1   Be brief and direct. There's no need to give convoluted explanations, just outline what you think would work for you and then stay quiet.
2   Be caring. Don't demand different behaviour – turn the situation round and ask yourself how your request (or something similar!) would sound to you.
3   Thank your partner for listening. Wait patiently for their response.

The majority of men welcome the chance to be a better lover to their partner and to experience deeper levels of love and passion with her. Lacking mind-reading skills, how are they to achieve this if they have absolutely no guidance?

By the way, when you are giving to your partner, rather than receiving, it's good to ask questions but again, keep it simple, along the lines of:

1   Would you like more pressure?
2   Would you like is faster/slower?
3   Where else would you like me to touch?

Don't ask complicated, multiple-choice type questions because they mean your partner has to think too much. Equally 'Do you like this?' and 'Does this feel good?' can be a bad idea because your partner may have to give a negative reply and then worry that this will wreck the moment. Allow your partner to give easy answers without having to agonize about hurting your feelings.

One of the joys of Tantra is that there should always be an element of fun between you, and if you are a woman who still thinks asking for what she would like in bed will make you sound like the power-crazed love child of Margaret Thatcher and Napoleon, try playing the following game.

The Yes, No, Maybe, Please Game

It is called the Yes, No, Maybe, Please Game, and to play it you simply do as the title suggests. When you have created a relaxing Tantric space (see Chapter Six), you take it in turns to play for anything between five minutes and half an hour. **One person is the recipient and the other is the doer.** The doer has to touch, stroke or massage the recipient somewhere on their body, and **the recipient has to give the feedback:** 'Yes', 'No', 'Maybe', or 'Please', depending on their reaction to the touch. **Then you swap over as many times as you like.** You can play this lying down or standing up, but lying down is more fun.

For a woman especially, this is an ideal way to set your boundaries, to help you say Yes and No and also to give positive feedback to your partner as to what you like. After all, until you can say a true 'no', your 'yes' doesn't mean very much, does it?

From a male point of view, the 'Yes, No' game can also be an eye-opener to the nature of a woman's skin, which scientists have demonstrated is up to ten times more sensitive than the skin of most men. For a woman to want to be touched is biologically natural. Considerable doses of the hormone oxytocin are released in women during sex, which arouses the desire to be stroked and cuddled. So if you are a woman who yearns for cuddles and doesn't get enough (or any), you can gently explain to your partner that some more touching would help satisfy a deep-seated biological need …

RACHEL, 34, LECTURER

'To be gently stroked all over gives me tingles all over my body. It can be the most beautiful and erotic sensation. For me it can be as pleasurable as normal sex. Sometimes a lot more so.'

The importance of sensual touch, sometimes gently teasing, sometimes firmer and more massaging, is greatly overlooked in our Western model of lovemaking. Tantrics often introduce feathers and other soft, velvety fabrics which can be lovingly trailed over their partner's skin. According to the Hindu love manual, the Ananga Ranga, the areas of a woman that need to be stroked are the head, eyes, lips, mouth, cheeks, ears, throat, nape of the neck, breasts, nipples, belly, back, arms, hands, thighs, knees, ankles, feet, vulva, waist, buttocks, the crown of the head and the centre of the forehead. Pretty much everywhere, in fact.

But if you are reading this with a view to pleasing your female partner, remember that some women prefer certain areas to be touched and not others. Check first. If stroking your partner's big toe reduces her to a state of ticklish hysteria, saying it's suggested in the Ananga Ranga won't help. If you really don't know where to begin, bear in mind that the line of a woman's spine, from the back of her neck to the cleft between her buttocks is well supplied with nerve endings and usually craves attention.

TAKE TIME TO TOUCH

Taking time to touch is part of a Tantric attitude to the needs of the woman, which reduces the Western emphasis on the race towards orgasm. According to Tantra teacher John, this slower approach often rings bells with women who are attracted by the idea of Tantra:

'In a sense, Tantra is stepping back into a more feminine way of experiencing the universe. After initial anxiety about what Tantra might mean, women usually say "Yes, this is my world; I have known this all the time". Women have their perception of a sexual relationship, which is about intimacy and sharing, being honoured, rather than being tied to the usual Western experience of sex which is more limited and concerned with releasing physical and emotional tensions.'

The female experience of orgasm

Not only do women experience orgasms differently from men, they experience them differently from other women. Equally, the same woman will have different orgasmic experiences at different times, depending on her physical, mental and emotional state. The amount of stimulation needed to generate an orgasm usually has very little to do with how much a woman enjoys sex.

Tantrics believe that as the sexual energy rises through the body it travels through the seven chakras, or energy centres (see page 24) activating each one in turn. This store of energy is not only physically pleasurable, but can take people into a state of emotional release and move them beyond their own individual personality into a merged and unfettered state. This is the transcendant, spiritual aspect of Tantra that goes way beyond the notion that it's simply about better bonking.

Orgasmic energy carries a vibration that is akin to the life force of all living things. In Tantra, once you have fully explored orgasm sexually, you can carry this powerful, creative energy into your everyday life, whether you are writing a novel or doing the washing up. Western sex tends to be about tension and release prior to rest. Tantric sex releases energy that transforms your existence for hours or even days.

Even though they may not have developed it, all women have a virtually limitless potential for orgasm. Most can achieve orgasm by masturbating, but some require no genital stimulation at all – they can simply build up to an orgasm through pleasurable feelings elsewhere in the body and mind. There are women who can come while on horseback; while riding on a tube train or when their partner kisses the back of their neck. I've heard of one woman who had her first orgasm as a teenager by having her hair brushed, and hairbrushing still presses the right buttons for her at 40.

But there is a fairly long list of stuff that can get in the way, including being annoyed or angry with your partner; stress (most people tend to have more sex on holiday); taking certain drugs (antihistamines and a huge array of other drugs will defuse your libido); smoking (chemicals in tobacco constrict blood flow to the genitals and may lower the level of testosterone in both men and women) – and being Catholic (nearly 60 per cent of Protestant women report that they nearly always have an orgasm during sex, while only 26 per cent of Catholic women do). This is possibly as a result of the Catholic Church's stand against masturbation, which is how a lot of women learn to have orgasms.

British sex guru Philip Hodson believes that lack of sexual desire is usually triggered by psychological anxiety. There can be a host of other reasons including a traumatic sexual experience as a child or teenager – rape, indecent assault or incestuous experience; an experience of 'ruptured intimacy', which might mean a bereavement, divorce, or family break-up. Although you may long for closeness, you can also feel threatened by it.

Equally, intimacy itself can bring its own anxieties – some people unconsciously see their partner as a reincarnated 'parent', especially after the birth of a baby, which may well be a turn-off. One partner can 'outgrow' the other after a period of years and sexual feelings lose their focus. If your sexual advances are frequently rejected, you may find that they cool after a while. Equally, having repetitive sex and doing exactly the same thing time after time with your partner can invite staleness into a sexual relationship. And a shock, such as grief that leads to depression, can eradicate sexual desire altogether.

The joy of Tantra is that it does not depend on an urge for frantic lovemaking leading to a genital orgasm for people to feel their sex life is complete. Tantra is about a union of two people that is not solely connected with their existence as sexual beings, but a connection between people at their highest and most loving level. You can leave behind worries about whether your will or won't come and concentrate on what is pleasurable for you right at this moment, rather than starting to make love with the pleasure of orgasm as a critical but distant objective.

The full-body orgasm

While Western sex focuses attention on the genitals during orgasm, the Tantric approach is different. Tantrics enjoy something known as a 'full-body orgasm', which means that the intense feelings associated with a genital orgasm are diffused through the entire body.

Instead of the rapid sense of release that comes with ordinary orgasm, energy can undulate through your entire body in wave-like pulsations, ranging from slight to strong tremors. People who have experienced a full-body orgasm often describe it as a kind of melting into themselves and their partner.

Tantra teacher Leora recommends the following exercise to cultivate a full-body orgasm:

1 Allow your sexual energy to rise higher and higher while you simultaneously and consciously relax into the pleasure and excitement. Notice how the sensations spread throughout your body.

2 At the point of orgasm, let your mind become still and quiet. Don't think about the orgasm. Simply relax throughout your body. Let your muscles relax, breath deeply and slowly, open your eyes, and look into your partner's eyes.

3 Let the orgasm have its way with you. Remember to keep breathing deeply and slowly, and to relax rather than tense your muscles. Your body may vibrate or shake and you may feel out of control. This is the beginning of a full-body orgasm.

Says Leora:

'I hadn't had a really satisfying sexual relationship before I started Tantra. I had a boyfriend who was known in our circle of friends and supposed to be a good lover, and although our relationship was sexually exciting, it wasn't fulfilling, there was a real sense of intimacy missing for me. I thought there was something wrong with me, because I wasn't having as much fun as he was having. I was left thinking 'What was all that about?'

Then I went on a Tantra course and I saw that the difference in approach was phenomenal. There was much more of a sense of slowness, of being in the moment and finding the experience of sexuality as a meeting. The pace and the quality were significantly different. I had a sense of being taken care of as a woman. The goal of making love was not just to ejaculate in the fastest and most exciting way; there was more to it than that.'

It is
possible to
spread your
sexual
energy
through
your body
rather than
experiencing
it being
released in
one 'quick'
orgasm

If you would like to experiment with making your orgasms more intense, here are a couple of other techniques that you may like to try. The first is to build up the excitement several times before you let yourself go ahead with the orgasm. When you feel very aroused, stop moving, contract your PC muscles and visualize energy going up your spine. Then begin to move again. Repeat this several times. Using this approach, you should reach successively higher levels of arousal. When you do finally reach orgasm, it should be an explosive experience.

It is also possible to spread your sexual energy through your body rather than experiencing it being released in one 'quick' orgasm. To do this, simply stop moving just before you reach orgasm. Breathe deeply into the sex and navel area

Orgasm can dispel period pains as it reduces cramps (though few mothers recommend it to their daughters) and Taoism has some splendid exercises to practise if you have problem periods

and imagine your sexual energy travelling into every cell of your body. Feel yourself warmly wrapped up in love, and sense your connectedness to your partner. You can stop for as long as 10 to 15 minutes. If you feel the fire of arousal begin to fade, you can make love again and repeat the process. Slowly your entire body will begin to feel different. Contrary to popular belief, relaxing rather than tensing helps people feel more and not less, and to feel it for a longer time. Enjoy!

ONLY WOMEN BLEED

'Only women bleed', as the Alice Cooper song goes. Menstruation is a subject that rarely comes up in books on improving your sexual relationships. While it is true that some women are not interested in sex while they are menstruating (and some are inwardly relieved that their period gives them an opportunity to turn down sex), menstruation is not a barrier to making love. According to sex expert Paul Johannides: 'Intercourse with a menstruating woman sometimes feels extra-nice for the following reasons:

1   The vagina might be super-lubricated due to menstrual secretions.
2   The added menstrual swelling might help a woman have a really nice orgasm.
3   Some women get extra-horny during their periods. This might be to do with a change in hormones, or perhaps they feel more relaxed since it's harder to get pregnant, although pregnancy is still a risk.'

Orgasm can dispel period pains as it reduces cramps (though few mothers recommend it to their daughters) and Taoism has some splendid exercises to practise if you have problem periods. The use of 'exercising eggs' which are usually solid marble or jade and which have a string attached to them is outlined in Mantak Chia's book, *Cultivating Female Sexual Energy*. The idea is that an egg is inserted vaginally and the woman uses her PC muscles to let it drop and then pull it back up the vaginal vault. This increases her awareness of her muscles and builds strength in them at the same time. You need to wash the egg thoroughly before and afterwards with hot soapy water. It is also advisable to run the egg under warm water first to warm it up. Here's one woman's story:

KATE, 24, STUDENT
'For as long as I can remember, my periods were a nightmare. My breasts were tender, the powerful painkillers my doctor prescribed made me vomit and I used to miss a week at university nearly every month because I felt so ill. Saying I had my period sounded like such a pathetic excuse, but I felt terrible. Then I read Mantak Chia's book, Cultivating Female Sexual Energy, *and I decided to try and practise the egg exercise he describes because I was so desperate to get some relief.*

I bought a jade egg, tied a bit of string through it, and started to move energy around my body by contracting the vaginal muscles while the egg was inside me. The first couple of times

I did it, some red stuff came out when I went to the loo. I thought it was the start of my period, but it wasn't. The next period I had was completely different. It was just amazing. The pain had gone; there was just a nice warm feeling in my pelvis and no discomfort at all. I've been fine for the past seven months since I began to practise the exercise, and my menstrual cycle now seems to coincide with the waxing and waning of the moon.
I have also begun to think differently about myself as a woman and to feel more positive about my periods. The experience has certainly changed my perceptions about my body.'

Periods tend to be something most women moan about or simply put up with; very few women actually celebrate this regular sign of their fertility and womanliness. Tantric texts, on the other hand, credit making love to a menstruating partner with the power of rejuvenation.

If you want to make love during your period, positions that allow the woman to go on top are the best, as they allow a downward flow. Lying on your back isn't a good idea because the menstrual flow is restricted and according to Tantra this can be harmful for the woman.

In her book, *Divine Sex*, yoga teacher Caroline Aldred advocates an entirely different approach to menstruation from the one common among most Western women. She suggests trying a ritual that can be performed alone or with your partner and involves placing your finger inside your vagina and dotting your forehead with a spot of your menstrual blood. She says: 'Give yourself time to meditate afterwards, or to sit quietly without distraction, or perform the ritual before you go to sleep at night. My lover and I share this ritual and, for us, the effects are quite profound. Being able to share the power of this experience with a partner who is open to view the woman with reverence and awe, understanding and respect, is a very purifying and powerful act, not to be abused.'

If just reading this makes you squirm in horror, hang on a moment and ask yourself why you find this suggestion so upsetting. Admittedly, this kind of ritual could be considered rather extreme and it certainly won't appeal to everyone, but the intention behind it – appreciating a solely female bodily function as something special and deserving respect – is admirable.

Resting in harmony

Back in 1947, Dr Rudolph Van Urban, an American doctor and sexologist, researched the stream of bioelectrical energy which is stimulated during sex for his book, *Sex Perfection and Marital Happiness*. He discovered that after 20 to 30 minutes of lying together, lovers would create an energy field that could reduce stress and high blood pressure, and help cure insomnia, ulcers and heart problems.

I'm not sure quite how he analysed all this scientifically, but even if the science is a little uncertain, the point he makes is a good one. Lying in the arms of someone you love for a decent amount of time creates a harmony between you that can flow into the rest of your life. It is harder to get wound up about the petty stuff and angry with your partner when you have just spent a blissful half hour (or more) together.

4

MEN
AND TANTRA

The idea that it's possible for a man to experience an orgasm without ejaculating is practically unknown in the West. If you try suggesting that men are capable of being multi-orgasmic, it's likely you'll meet blank stares of disbelief. In fact, it's relatively straightforward for a man to experience an orgasm without ejaculation and to become multi-orgasmic. Tantra teaches you how to do both.

Both Tantra and the Tao share an approach to sexuality that is very different from the one that is prevalent in the West. If you are a man, you may well be wondering why you should even consider a new way of looking at your sexual relationships. After all, most men say that orgasm is one of the most pleasurable physical sensations on earth. Why give up this immensely enjoyable and satisfying experience as the goal of your lovemaking?

The short answer is that you don't have to. This book isn't about forcing people to abandon the good things that are currently in their lives. Its purpose is to inform them of the other exciting and fulfilling options that are on offer. After all, according to Tantra teacher John, Tantra is about choice:

'Tantra does not prescribe and say "This is right and this is wrong". You can still enjoy a quickie, or what I think the writer Erica Jong called the "zipless fuck", if that is what you and your partner want at the time. But Tantra teaches you about connection and becoming aware of what is happening in terms of the energy flow between you.

For a man, almost everything can change with the idea that you don't penetrate a woman, she receives you. So you don't use sex to relieve your stress over the fact that your boss was down on you or whatever else; women are not dustbins. You connect with your partner's heart, and as you do this you build a strong energetic connection so that love flows back into you. And instead of losing something by ejaculating fast to get rid of your stress, you receive something much more powerful and positive.

Rather than regarding relationships as a game which you have to somehow play and win, you stop manipulating and go with the energy flow. Tantra teaches you a sensitivity and responsiveness that women appreciate on a very deep level.'

What a lot of men don't realise is that they are born with the capacity of a Ferrari; they have the power, the responsiveness and the excitement of driving in a top-of-the-range supercar at their fingertips, if only they understood a little more about the extra buttons on the dashboard

So not only can you choose to be multi-orgasmic, you can bring much more pleasure and excitement to your partner.

JAMES, 45, ELECTRICIAN

'If you've only got five minutes before you dash out the door, a quickie is fine. But Tantra has opened up the possibility of choice for me. You can give and receive pleasure without the goal of ejaculation and it can open out into two or three hours of languid, luxuriant lovemaking. I've learnt to focus solely on receiving pleasure and then on giving pleasure. It is an altogether different dimension of lovemaking. I'm totally hooked.'

ORGASM IS NOT THE SAME AS EJACULATION

Let's stick to basics for a while and look at the mechanics of male sexuality. The male body is capable of a lot more than the majority of men think. Most men treat their body as though it's a Nissan Micra; it's fairly reliable and it gets them from A to B – or from the beginning of sex to their destination of orgasm – usually without breaking down. The ride may be OK, or more than OK, but it's getting to the destination that really matters.

What a lot of men don't realise, however, is that they are born with the capacity of a Ferrari; they have the power, the responsiveness and the excitement of driving in a top-of-the-range supercar at their fingertips, if only they understood a little more about the extra buttons on the dashboard. If there were a driver's manual for the male body, one of the most crucial nuggets of information would be that orgasm is not the same as ejaculation.

The full-body orgasm

Tantric practice encourages men to learn to delay ejaculation and to experience a series of 'full-body' orgasms rather than treating the 'normal' six-second, genitally located male orgasm as the goal of sex. Every man's experience is different, but the description below may give you some indication of what it can be like:

Mike, 42, management consultant

'I was persuaded by my wife to go on a Tantric workshop and, mainly to keep her happy, I agreed. The exercises that we did seemed pleasant enough, and then on the Sunday morning we were talked through something the teacher called 'The firebreath orgasm'. I lay down on the floor and went along with it, thinking I'd just go through the motions. I was fully dressed for a start, and if someone had said to me, "You can have an orgasm without a partner, without ejaculating and with your clothes on," I would probably have replied, "Don't be a wanker!" The teacher had said something about using the "fake it til you make it" technique if we weren't sure about how much we were getting out of the exercises so, as I didn't really think it was possible, that's what I decided to do. I'd heard of the chakras and the fact that you could move energy between them, but I had never experienced anything myself to support the idea that you can feel energy moving inside your body. I thought it was just people talking it up, or perhaps they'd felt a little twinge and claimed, "That's energy moving between my chakras!"

The Tantra teacher talked us through it over background music and told us to touch different parts of our bodies after we had spent a few minutes rocking the pelvis, working from the base chakra up. I went along with this for about ten minutes and then the first thing I noticed was that I was getting hotter and hotter. It was a really nice heat, centred in my chest.

I actually felt as though there was a rush of something going through my body. It was like gravel or sand passing up and down a tube – a kind of whooshing sensation. I had never felt anything like it before.

Then I started to convulse in the way that you do in a normal orgasm, but it was all over my body. It built up and went on for ages. I wasn't aware of time, but from the beginning of the really pleasurable experience, which I could equate with an orgasm, to the end, it felt like 15 to 20 minutes at least. All I was doing was breathing and focusing on my body and it was creating the most incredible feelings.

We were told to breathe the energy between the chakras, but I experimented with different ways of being aware of the sensations in my body. I rested one hand on one area of my body and moved the other hand over my body as I breathed in, but by the time I got to the top – the point between your eyebrows and the crown of the head – the sensations were so intense and amazing that I felt I was on the ceiling.

After 15 minutes into the exercise I had to get up and leave the room to have a pee. The orgasm itself hadn't started then, but I was having such nice experiences that my legs were wobbly, and I found it very difficult to balance. I remember supporting myself along the wall as I walked out of the room to the loo, and staggering like I was drunk. It was a lot like having a bottle of wine. I've never had to pee halfway through making love, so I can't say what level of coordination I would normally have in those circumstances. By the time I came back to start again, my arousal had dropped a bit, but not much, say from 70 per cent to 50 per cent, but it very quickly went back up. Within a minute it was back up to 70 per cent and then it just carried on going upwards. The experience became so intense that I didn't really want it to finish. If you are a man and you think of that moment just at ejaculation, and it might last for a couple of seconds, that is how intense it was, but it was expanded over a long period of time and it could have run and run.

Because I was in a workshop I was aware that things had gone quiet round me and I needed to come back into the room. Someone came and held my feet and that grounded me and I knew that I had to stop. I still felt very sharp and yet relaxed for hours afterwards. Quite bouncy, in fact, which is a very different experience to the "I'd like to roll over and go to sleep now" sort of feeling that I get sometimes.

I think I was in some sort of trance, but at the same time I was thinking very clearly. It was one of the main differences between a full-body orgasm and a normal orgasm when you ejaculate with a partner. I felt quite euphoric after this. Maybe because it was the best orgasm I'd ever had – I have to admit I felt quite tearful at the end of it, but they were literally tears of joy.

I really want to learn how to incorporate it into lovemaking with my partner. That would be great. I wouldn't say I could go on all night, because I guess you would get tired at some point, but I could certainly imagine myself doing it for hours rather than minutes. It took me to a place I had never been before. It was the highest high I've ever experienced.'

Taoism, which is a sexual practice closely linked to Chinese medicine, advocates non-ejaculation primarily for its health benefits, since the doctors of ancient China believed that men lived healthier and longer lives by retaining their semen or the body's 'life-force'. I have included Tantric and Taoist techniques in this chapter; try out whichever appeals most to you.

More than 60 years ago, the pioneering US sex researcher, Alfred Kinsey, reported that men were capable of being multi-orgasmic, but for some reason this knowledge scarcely made it into public consciousness, possibly because so few men understood exactly how to make it happen.

Perhaps surprisingly, it is not especially difficult. According to Tao master Mantak Chia:

'Since orgasm and ejaculation generally occur within seconds of one another, it is easy to confuse them. To become multi-orgasmic, you must learn the ability to separate the different sensations of arousal and to revel in orgasm without cresting over into ejaculation … Unlike orgasm, which is a peak emotional and physical experience, ejaculation is simply a reflex that occurs at the base of the spine and results in the ejection of semen.'

Yet trying to convince some men that ejaculation is just an involuntary muscle spasm, and as such need play no part in orgasm, is not easy. Women can have trouble accepting this too:

MATT, 29, MUSICIAN
'One girlfriend who wasn't into Tantra didn't like the fact that I didn't ejaculate. She thought I was holding something back, and it made her feel uncomfortable. It helps if you're both on the same wavelength when you practise this.'

In fact, the process of non-ejaculation is designed to bring a couple closer together, not drive them apart. Tantrics believe that by not ejaculating, a man can move his sexual energy around his body, leaving him able to continue to make love with his partner for as long as they both like. This means he need never suffer from the sense of feeling 'wiped out' that so many men experience after ejaculation. It also means that his partner is not suddenly left to her own devices while her exhausted man drifts off to solitary sleep.

Comedians may hold up the bloke who ejaculates, grunts and snores in the space of a couple of minutes as a figure of fun, but the audience's laughter is based on a recognition of what goes on in bedrooms up and down the country. Five thousand years ago, Peng-Tze, a sex counsellor to the Chinese Yellow Emperor reported, 'After ejaculating, a man is tired, his ears buzz, his eyes are heavy, and he longs for sleep. He is thirsty and his limbs feel weak and stiff. In ejaculating he enjoys a brief moment of sensation but then suffers long hours of exhaustion.'

CONTROLLING EJACULATION

The ancient Taoist masters, who were originally doctors, noted that ejaculation drained a man of vital energy. They pointed to Nature, where plants die or become dormant once they give their seed (hence the English expression 'gone to seed' describing someone or something that has pretty much fallen apart). They suggested that a man should limit the number of times he ejaculates, according to his age and state of health – unless, of course, he wanted to conceive a child.

Modern Taoists remain confident that ejaculating harms a man's health. They point out that an average ejaculation contains 50 million to 250 million sperm cells. Every one of these cells is capable of creating half a new human being. Your body assumes it is getting ready to create new life and according to the Tao, all the

Tantrics, meanwhile, urge that a man should delay the urge to ejaculate not only to give him more time to bring greater pleasure to his partner, but to experience multiple and full-body orgasms

A mere repetition of the sexual act, in all its variations, is not Tantra. If this were so, then Casanova would have been a great Tantric master. In actual fact, Casanova, Don Juan and the other legendary lovers of the Western world would have been held in the greatest contempt by the Tantrists of their age organs and glands in your body give their best possible energy – 'orgasmic energy' – to this worthy cause. However, most people make love for pleasure far more times than they do for procreation. As a result, men lose precious energy that could be used to strengthen their minds and bodies.

This is a controversial view. There are Western scientists who would say that the amount of vitamins and nutrients lost by a man when he ejaculates is minimal and easily replaced. But there are also more than a few Western men who agree that ejaculation takes the edge off their performance outside the bedroom. There are still plenty of athletes, for example, who fear that sex may drain them of vital energy and as a result don't make love before a big match. Whether wives and girlfriends should accompany the English football or cricket teams when they go on tour is a subject still hotly debated in the tabloid press. So perhaps the Taoist masters had a point …

Tantrics, meanwhile, urge that a man should delay the urge to ejaculate not only to give him more time to bring greater pleasure to his partner, but to experience multiple and full-body orgasms. The main difference with these is that instead of the intense and immediate release that happens when ejaculation occurs, they offer a way of relaxing into physical, emotional and even spiritual sensations which are then magnified throughout the whole body.

Matt, 29, musician

'When you have ejaculatory sex you reach a certain point and then it's over. Using these techniques keeps the pleasure getting higher and higher. I don't get that same short burst of intensity that I achieve with ejaculation, but then I don't go crashing down and feel wiped out afterwards. Instead I feel really good and full of energy. I'd say it's a thousand per cent better, honestly.'

Priyatama, 52, sex therapist

'I work as a sex therapist, and men tend to be very goal-orientated both in the workplace and in their sex lives. They say things like "I get turned on sexually and before I know it I've ejaculated, and there wasn't much in it for me or my partner". And they get incredibly

anxious about doing it right. Tantra offers them the framework to slow down. Tantra is not about performance; it's about individuality. It's about exploration, and it offers a way of being more intimate, more playful and, almost above all, more relaxed. Finding this out can be such a relief for men. It lifts a burden from their shoulders.'

According to Indian Tantric experts Arvind and Shanta Kale:

'One of the first victims of Western man's unseemly haste is his sex life. Efficiency is measured by the speed with which a person completes an act effectively, and an effective act of sex is an act which results in orgasm … In other words, the quicker the orgasm the more effective the intercourse. This strange perversion of values has resulted in us glorifying the male who can copulate with the greatest number of females and the female who is most willing to forego the delightful preliminaries of civilized sex.

A mere repetition of the sexual act, in all its variations, is not Tantra. If this were so, then Casanova would have been a great Tantric master. In actual fact, Casanova, Don Juan and the other legendary lovers of the Western world would have been held in the greatest contempt by the Tantrists of their age. To the Tantrist the West lays unreasonable emphasis on the quantity of sex; the more women a man copulates with the more heroic he becomes in the eyes of society. Tantrists believe that such sexual performances are criminal wastes of the sexual powers.

Men nowadays embark on sex with the wrong ideas. We firmly believe that every act of Tantric sex must be a seduction, sometimes by the man, at other times by the woman.'

In their book, *Tantra, The Secret Power of Sex*, the Kales go on to outline an approach to sex that is prefaced by an hour or two of different types of kissing (there are 19 different varieties of kiss outlined in the Kama Sutra, after all) and intercourse in which a man should be able to make love for a minimum of 30 minutes (preferably 90) before ejaculation.

Of course, you may not choose to do this. If you're exhausted by work, worn out by the kids and you have to be up early the next morning, you may regard a ten-minute cuddle that ends another ten minutes later with ejaculatory sex as a major achievement. On the other hand, if a brief coupling every now and then is all your love life amounts to, you may be interested in at least finding out how to move it on to a more rewarding level.

The techniques that will allow you to do this (and more) are described later in this chapter, but first it's useful to analyse why Western men have orgasm and ejaculation so inextricably linked in their minds as signs of virility and manliness.

One of the main culprits is the pornography industry, which portrays a one-dimensional view of sex that is visually exciting to men (and plenty of women), but bears as much resemblance to the physical and emotional sexual responses of real people as a crocodile to a handbag: only the skin is the same.

For most young boys in the West, porn films or magazines are one of their first introductions to women in the context of sex. Yet they offer misleading information. Firstly, they usually portray men thrusting away, in a sawing rhythm that is a recipe for fast ejaculation and little satisfaction for either the man or the woman. In fact, the fast thrusting that goes on in the average porn film is timed more to the masturbatory rhythm of a man's hand than anything based on the sensual subtleties that accompany the best kind of real-life sex.

Next, in porn-land, the female partner screams in ecstasy (suggesting that this frantic thrusting is what women love – they might, but only sometimes and only when it's linked to other sexually stimulating behaviour). And finally, much is made of the ejaculation inside or outside the woman and it's generally accomplished with great bravado and a burst of Beethoven's 'Ode to Joy' (well, almost). A Real Man in porn films can ejaculate again and again. But it's the equivalent of expecting onlookers to be impressed when you choke on a stray piece of popcorn at the cinema – ejaculation is simply a bodily reflex. It is not integral to the orgasmic response.

And it's not just pornography that gives convoluted messages about sex. Most Hollywood films offer a modified version of the same thing. Film actress Candice Bergen described her formula for being on the receiving end of pump-and-grind movie sex in *Esquire* magazine: 'Ten seconds of heavy breathing, roll your head from side to side, simulate a slight asthma attack, and die a little.' It's no surprise that so many young men fantasize about being taught how to make love properly by an older woman; a Mrs Robinson figure lingers in the psyche of countless males.

Tantra, however, teaches you how to make love on an entirely different plain from the narrow version depicted in pornography or Hollywood. The difference can be summed up succinctly: porn succeeds when it takes you into another world of someone else's pleasure. That may be fine and on occasion exactly what you are looking for. But Tantra enables you to go inwards and experience your own pleasure.

WOMEN DON'T ALWAYS WANT A PENIS ...

John Gray's books on male/female relationships have sold millions of copies all over the world, and contain plenty of good advice. But I'd urge caution before you adopt his recommendation that every so often women should grant their men three to five-minute 'quickie' sex, simply to keep their partners sexually satisfied. (This is on the understanding that both sides will make time for longer sex at another time.)

It's difficult to see how women can become turned-on under these circumstances. Generally, women want to feel admired and desired. There's not much to be said for being on the receiving end of a brief burst of someone else's masturbation. There is also a danger that unless the woman uses lots of lubricant, she will probably be physically uncomfortable and, some sex experts believe, more likely to succumb to vaginal bruising and infections as a result.

If you both want a quickie, that's fine. But if a woman is going along with it simply so the man can get his urge to ejaculate out of the way, from a Tantric perspective there will be little benefit to the relationship. Generally speaking, women want intimacy and honouring. The idea of a woman granting sex in order to get something else (whether it's better sex at a later time or a new kitchen) sounds perilously close to prostitution. Tantra is the opposite of this. It is about connection and respect.

women don't always want a penis

Tantra also teaches that the sexual satisfaction of the woman is important. Certainly not at the expense of her male partner, but it is a different story from the 'smash and grab' attitude of men who cling to the Victorian attitude that women aren't really sexual creatures and a chap has to get as much sex as he can when it's on offer. Thankfully, this view is held only by a minority. Research supports the fact that most men think differently. One US survey of 4,000 men reported that 80 per cent judged their own sexual satisfaction by whether they had been able to give their partner one or more orgasms.

MAKE GIVING PLEASURE YOUR GOAL

Although this is excellent news for women, perhaps this is a suitable moment to point out to male readers that when you travel down the road to becoming a better lover, orgasms are not something you can 'give' to a woman. Go down that route and you stumble across the boulders of analysing your sexual performance as though it were a sports match. It's much more useful to hold in mind the Tantric idea that you want to give your partner as much pleasure as possible, and to enjoy as much pleasure as you can yourself. That way no woman will ever feel under pressure to fake an orgasm just to make you happy and meet your expectations; she can relax and enjoy herself (and so can you).

According to US sex therapist, Dr Laura Berman, co-author of *For Women Only*:

'There's a huge pressure from men on women to reach orgasm every time. Women want orgasms too, but female orgasms are much more loaded for men than for women. Even the most sexually functional women don't reach orgasm every time – only 30 per cent of women reach orgasm through intercourse. That's why so many women fake it, so that their men don't feel like they are bad lovers or that they're not real men.

If a woman is feeling attended to, understood, appreciated, helped, supported, cared for, stimulated; all those things are aphrodisiacs. A lot of men don't know that washing the dishes or giving the kids breakfast so his partner can take a bath or read the paper are some of the biggest aphrodisiacs he can provide.'

Most women would say that the best lovers are the ones who are comfortable in their own skin, relaxed, and aware of what is going on in their bodies and in their partner's body. They are also much more likely to be fun. A man who is single-mindedly obsessed with 'making' a woman have an orgasm is not the kind of lover most women want in their beds.

SUSIE, 40, CHEF

'I get a bit panicky when a boyfriend starts acting like he's expecting me to come. Some men think if they push certain buttons you'll be programmed to have an orgasm, but it's not like that. And just because it's worked the time before, it doesn't mean they can repeat the same pattern and get the same result. But when a man acts like he only wants to give me a good time, and he really cares about me on all sorts of levels, that's when I'm more likely to have an orgasm and I feel like I want to do everything I can for him too. It becomes a genuine two-way flow, instead of "I'll do this for you, so I expect you to do this for me".'

Female sexual satisfaction mattered to the ancient Tantrics and Taoists because the woman was considered an open channel of life-giving forces. Because in the Taoist tradition man is fire and woman is water, their sexual responses were acknowledged as different. A man's sexual energy heats up quickly and then explodes; a woman's is more like a pan of cool water coming to the boil: it heats and cools slowly (and can simmer for ages!) So men have to learn to match their partner's different rate of arousal if each is to reach an ecstatic peak of pleasure that is both healing and inspirational.

JAMES, 45, ELECTRICIAN

'Giving up the idea that I had to make my partner have an orgasm before I had an orgasm and concentrating on our mutual pleasure and hanging out in that space instead was a big step forward for me. Also, changing my viewpoint and trying to see my partner as a goddess, as the essence of the female, rather than as a sex object, broadened my understanding of male and female sexuality. I learnt the importance of honouring the other person, rather than

The ability to delay ejaculation is an essential part of a great lover's toolkit for stimulating pleasure in a woman. A lot of women take longer to reach arousal than a man. By delaying his ejaculation, the man can let her reach levels of arousal to match his, instead of making her feel that somehow she has to hurry to catch up *seeing them as a source of quick thrills. Tantra has given me a set of tools to do this, and my whole life, not just my sex life, is so much richer as a result.'*

Although suggesting a shift in the balance between male and female along more Tantric lines sounds like a reversal of the Western attitude to sex, it is actually more in tune with what most 21st-century men really believe. Men enjoy giving pleasure to women and for the majority, a highly turned-on woman is a huge turn-on for them. It gives a healthy boost to their sexual confidence when their partner is clearly enjoying herself and is noisily appreciative of their lovemaking skills.

The ability to delay ejaculation is an essential part of a great lover's toolkit for stimulating pleasure in a woman. A lot of women take longer to reach arousal than a man. By delaying his ejaculation, the man can let her reach levels of arousal to match his, instead of making her feel that somehow she has to hurry to catch up.

There are two points to remember here. The first is that it is easier for a man to learn to become multi-orgasmic if he is already in a close and loving relationship that allows plenty of time for leisurely lovemaking. However, if you're not in a relationship, don't worry – you can still explore your potential for learning this skill on your own. In fact, some of the exercises that will enable you to achieve multiple orgasms are best practised alone before you try them out with your partner.

The second point is that you are unlikely to learn to do this in half an hour or even overnight (sorry about that). Mantak Chia, the guru of multi-orgasmic men, says that multiple orgasms take a week or two to master, and that perfecting the technique takes around six months. (Some British men say this is overly optimistic.) There will also be times when you fall over the edge into ejaculation and occasions when your urge to ejaculate is stronger than your desire to delay. This is only to be expected and is not something that you should beat yourself up about. These techniques require patience and practice. They are intended to give you a better time in bed and not to become a source of anxiety or stress. So don't let them. When things don't work out quite as you planned, accept that it is part of your learning curve, and enjoy whatever experience you have to its fullest.

KEERTI, 36, THERAPIST

'When I first found out about these techniques, I was like a mad scientist trying to explore it all. I think in the beginning I tried to impose my ability not to ejaculate on my girlfriends because it appealed to me in terms of what it meant to be a good lover. A kind of "I can go on for hours" guy and that fed my male ego. In hindsight there was a kickback to that which wasn't so great, because it was a control thing and some girlfriends didn't like it. I was being mechanical about it and that missed the point. I chucked the baby out with the bathwater.

Now I appreciate that sometimes it's nice just to have raw sex and sometimes it's good to relax and go with the flow. If I talk to other men about it, I suggest that they start off by giving themselves a set amount of time to explore this different way of making love, otherwise they freak out thinking "I've got to do this for hours and hours". And make the changes slowly, one at a time, and get used to the feel of it before trying something else. The best thing that Tantra has given me is the freedom to explore.'

The idea of delaying ejaculation is not new. The earliest cavemen probably mentally recited the names of the local dinosaur-baiting crew when they wanted to carry on making love for a few enjoyable minutes more. This method of distracting yourself from arousal is sometimes effective, but its end result can often be to take you out of your body and into your head, rather than allowing you to relax and enjoy what is going on in your body at any one time.

Similarly, a lot of men rely on drinking alcohol to slow them down in bed. Apart from the fact that being drunk will probably make you less sensitive to the sexual needs of your partner (and less popular as a result), alcohol is an anaesthetic and numbs sensation. So although it may dampen your arousal, it will also reduce your ability to control it. The art of multiple orgasms lies in knowing your personal arousal rate, not ignoring it. As you become more in tune with the rise in your sexual temperature, it will become easier for you to control it. You won't be able to do this if you've had too much to drink.

"There have been some occasions when we've been making love and I've relaxed into the energy and it has felt like the energy has come out of the top of my head. I know it's a hackneyed phrase, but it's been a cosmic experience. It may sound strange considering that I have given up the goal of ejaculation, but practising Tantra has made me much more aware of my masculinity. It sounds a bit airy fairy but it has given me a physical awareness of my body that I didn't have before."

The multiple orgasm

In order to understand how multiple orgasms work, first you need to know how the male orgasm is structured. According to the Taoists there are four stages of erection or 'attainments':

1 firmness (also referred to as lengthening)
2 swelling
3 hardness
4 heat (this is when your testicles draw into your body)

Western doctors also agree with these four stages, although they describe them in slightly different terms. It is much easier to avoid ejaculating when you can remain in the erect and hard third stage. According to Mantak Chia,

'The ejection of semen from your body actually occurs in two parts. In the contractile (sometimes called "emission") phase, the prostate contracts and empties semen into the urethra. In the expulsion phase, the semen is propelled down the urethra and out of the penis. When you become multi-orgasmic you will experience the pleasurable pelvic contractions – felt as a popping or fluttering sensation in your prostate – without actually ejaculating.'

During the contractile phase, you'll feel a series of prostate contractions lasting between three and five seconds. Though the intensity of these varies, and they can often be as intense as regular ejaculatory orgasms, at first they can be quite mild. Instead of carrying on to the point where you simply must ejaculate, hold still for a moment – long enough for you to gain control of your arousal state. You can also squeeze your PC muscle (the ring of muscle at the base of your pelvis described in Chapter Two), which will also give you some control over your prostate. At the same time (hey, you can manage this!) draw the sexual energy up your spine and away from your genitals. This may well lead to 'fireworks' or orgasmic feelings in your brain, other parts of your body or even your entire body. Welcome to the world of the whole-body orgasm!

JAMES, 45, ELECTRICIAN

'I never make love now with the perspective of going for an ejaculation or orgasm. Frankly, it's more enjoyable for me to focus on the pleasure and watch it build up and sink down and build up and sink down and stay with that pleasure and not have to worry about a goal. Although I have to say when my partner first suggested that I shouldn't aim for an orgasm I felt pretty angry. As a man I thought it was my birthright to ejaculate. But I agreed to try it when we made love; I knew that I could always ejaculate through masturbation anyway. Now I couldn't go back to the old way of making love. Quite often, when we finish making love, I'm still in a state of pleasure that stays inside me, sometimes for a day or so. I have more energy and more enthusiasm for what I'm doing, whether it's work or washing the dishes.

There have been some occasions when we've been making love and I've relaxed into the energy and it has felt like the energy has come out of the top of my head. I know it's a hackneyed phrase, but it's been a cosmic experience. It may sound strange considering that I have given up the goal of ejaculation, but practising Tantra has made me much more aware of my masculinity. It sounds a bit airy fairy but it has given me a physical awareness of my body that I didn't have before.'

When you are highly aroused, a few drops of clear fluid may drip out of your penis. The Taoists refer to this as 'water'; it is preseminal fluid that paves the way for the sperm and may contain a small number of sperm itself, which is what Family Planners warn about if you practise contraception by withdrawing from the vagina before ejaculation. This, say the Taoists, is distinguished from 'milk' or semen, which if you practise non-ejaculation properly is simply reabsorbed by the body.

WAYNE, 34, ANTIQUES RESTORER

'In my experience, it's quite easy to have multiple orgasms, but when you begin, they are not as intense as an orgasm that's linked to ejaculation. But with time and practice, it's as if the body becomes able to channel more orgasmic energy and they grow stronger and stronger. But you've got to give yourself plenty of time to make mistakes when you don't get your timing right and not beat yourself up about it. When I've talked to people about this approach to

sex, they go "Yeah, but ordinary sex is fantastic", but even though you have to make a bit more of an effort, this kind of sex is vastly superior. I could never go back to the old way of making love. Just having sex to ejaculate seems so primitive. An orgasm for me now is a total body experience, it's not just confined to my genitals. There's no comparison, really.'

CAN NON-EJACULATION BE HARMFUL?

According to the Taoists, quite the reverse is true. This technique has been practised for thousands of years with considerable benefits to the health and longevity of the men who practise it and no reported ill effects. (Mantak Chia must be a pensioner by now, but he looks about 40).

(The practice of non-ejaculation, by the way, is not the same as retrograde ejaculation – a medical condition when sperm enter the bladder during ejaculation instead of being expelled through the urethra and penis. The sperm are later flushed out with urine. This is very common after prostate surgery, but it can happen in anyone and is harmless.)

When you are approaching the idea of non-ejaculation for the first time, it's easy to see it as something involving a degree of loss. A willingness to try it does involve a change of mindset on the part of most men. But, as you'll experience when you try it out, the benefits greatly outweigh any difficulties you may have in getting used to a new way of doing things.

When you become more sensitive to the energy flow in your body, you will be able to draw it up your spine from your genitals, and move it down the front of your body in order to circulate the energy between you when you are making love. Taoist tradition says that by retaining and reabsorbing sexual fluids into your system, your sexual identity intensifies. This will make you more attractive and draw your partner to you, allowing a heightened intimacy between you. While this sounds like a worthwhile bonus, it's hard to quantify scientifically. My guess is that a man's partner is probably grateful to him for the effort he is making in bed if he masters these techniques for their mutual benefit, and it's her sense of appreciation that draws her to him and improves their relationship.

Wayne, 34, antiques restorer

'I used to feel a real drop in energy after ejaculation. It was like I had all the windows open and a heater on until my body restored itself. Now I move that powerful sexual energy round my body and pack it into other areas like my brain. I actually think well after achieving an orgasm without ejaculating now, although immediately afterwards I feel a great sense of stillness and pleasure. My girlfriend and I can keep building up towards orgasm again and again; it's like surfing over wave after wave of pleasure. Another person's body becomes an extension of your own.'

So how do you do it?

The basic semen retention techniques can be used singly or in combination, depending on your needs and your ability to master them. Try the following exercises for an idea of what non-ejaculation is all about. One word of advice – have a pee first. A full bladder will make you feel like you need to ejaculate and will make it more difficult if you want to stop.

Breathing

One of the bodily effects associated with ejaculation is a rapid increase in heart rate. If you can keep your heart rate as close as you can to normal, you will be able to delay your urge to ejaculate. One way of doing this is to take deep, rhythmic breaths that will reduce your heart rate and help you resist building the excitement to uncontrollable ejaculation. Practise the following breathing exercise:

1   Sit in a comfortable position, relax your shoulders and have your hands palms upwards on your knees. Take a few normal breaths.

2   Move the palms of your hands to your lower belly and place them on your abdomen.

3   Breathe in deeply through your nose so that you can feel your belly pushing out as you inhale.

4   Exhale fully (again through your nose) keeping your chest relaxed. Feel your belly move back towards your spine and be aware of your penis and testicles pulling up slightly.

5   Continue to inhale deeply and exhale deeply for nine, 18 or 36 times. Then
relax and breathe normally.

When practising this exercise, always inhale through your nose, which filters and warms the air. It is harder for your body to work with cold, unfiltered air that is taken in directly through the mouth.

Most of us suffer because our breathing is too shallow. This means we take in only a small amount of oxygen, which reduces our physical energy levels and allows toxins to build up in the body and weaken our resistance to disease. The average pair of lungs is capable of breathing in more than 3 litres (6 pints) of air; most people use less than a third of their total lung capacity when breathing normally. When you learn to control your breathing pattern, you are on the path to mastering the other bodily functions that will enable you to gain complete control over whether you choose to ejaculate or not.

SQUEEZING YOUR PC MUSCLE

The pubococcygeus muscle (see page 59) plays an important role in male ejaculation. The stronger it is, the better able you are to bring it into play when you don't want to come. You can exercise it whenever you choose. If you find yourself stuck in traffic or waiting for a train, pull up and release your PC muscle as often as you can. Alternatively, watching TV is an ideal occupation to combine with a PC muscle workout. Because the Taoists were particularly keen on their nine times table, and nearly all of the repetitions of their techniques are divisible by nine, they recommend doing this exercise, surprise, surprise, between 9 and 36 times.

SELF-PLEASURING

A good way of learning the technique of non-ejaculation is to start by practising it during masturbation. Astonishing as it may seem, as recently as 1994 Dr Jocelyn Elders, the US surgeon general, was forced to resign for stating publicly that masturbation 'is a part of human sexuality'. Certain religious and cultural taboos still linger around it. Nevertheless, research shows that these taboos do not deter the 80 to 95 per cent of men who regularly masturbate. The expressions referring to masturbation are many and varied and include: 'spanking the monkey', 'bashing the bishop' and – my personal favourite – 'strangling the one-eyed monster' ... 'Masturbation' sounds rather clinical and calling someone a wanker in Britain is an insult, so I've chosen the Tantric term 'self-pleasuring', which, if nothing else, should be an accurate description of what you are doing.

TEN STEPS TO PRACTISE SELF–PLEASURING

1 Just as if you were creating a special space for you and your partner to enjoy, light a candle, put on some soft music, make sure you won't be disturbed and turn the lights down low. This is not a prelude to a Barry White extravaganza (unless Barry White is the music maestro linked to your sexiest moments), but a chance for you to practise – and enjoy – an exercise that will enable you to delay or prevent ejaculation when you are with your partner. Men tend to rush during solo sex; either because they grew up without much privacy and they wanted to get it over without anyone walking in on them, or because they want to get to the orgasm as quickly as possible. When you begin this exercise, make sure you have plenty of time and no pressing engagements likely to distract you.

2 If you use pornography or erotica normally try, once you are aroused, to shift your attention to the sensations in your own body.

3 Lubricate your penis – this will enable you to be more aware of your physical sensations. Oil lasts longer than any type of lotion.

4 Stimulate your entire penis. Most men concentrate on the head, which is the most sensitive part. But the Taoists believe that the entire penis should be given a work out as the different parts of the penis correspond to different parts of the body (although I have yet to meet a penis reflexologist; it sounds like an interesting career).

5 Touch your testicles and explore your Million Dollar Point, or MDP (see page 58). Testicles can be especially sensitive to light touch (especially if your hand

You are

exploring

your sexuality

in a way that

many other men

miss out on.

You are well

on the path to

becoming a

multi-orgasmic

man and a

better lover

has not strayed below your penis before). Wait until you are highly aroused before you touch your MDP. If you don't feel any sensation, or if you don't like the feeling, stop and try again when you feel more turned-on. Pushing on the MDP and squeezing your PC muscle (see page 59) when you are about to ejaculate can help stop the ejaculatory reflex. Pushing it gently can send more blood into your penis, which will make it throb harder. Apply strong, rhythmic pressure if you want to simulate the prostate contractions that accompany the contractile-phase orgasm.

6 When you feel yourself getting close to the edge of ejaculating, almost to the point of no return, stop stimulating yourself and become still.

7 Relax your PC muscle, and breathe deeply and slowly.

8 Press your tongue against the top of your palate. This will move your energy around your body, away from the genital region and help delay ejaculation.

9 If you are able to experience the involuntary PC contractions that occur at contractile-phase orgasm, congratulations! It is easier to feel them if you relax into them rather than tense around them. Don't be disappointed if they don't set off fireworks at first. If you can relax, they will eventually spread throughout your body. Some men experience them as a series of pleasurable shivers.

10 After you regain control, start and stop again several times. You should feel peaceful or energised or both. If you crest over into ejaculation, don't feel you have failed. You are exploring your sexuality in a way that many other men miss out on. You are well on the path to becoming a multi-orgasmic man and a better lover.

If this sounds like a burdensome list of instructions, just try incorporating one or two suggestions in your usual routine before you put them all together. These techniques are about increasing pleasure, and that won't be the result if you feel under pressure. Equally, your partner may find it disappointing if you begin to count mastering these techniques as the most important thing when you make love.

ALAN, 34, COMPUTER PROGRAMMER

'I've been practising this on and off for about 18 months now and I wouldn't say that it's particularly easy. I found it required a heck of a lot of concentration when I started and I needed to fail a couple of times to realize where I was going wrong. I can stop ejaculation when I want to now, and I find the more I shift the sexual energy around my body, the more the desire to ejaculate decreases. I've been really busy with work lately, so it's not something I've devoted loads of time to, but I shall carry on the practice because I think it's good skill to have as a lover.'

Taoists say that sexual energy magnifies the energy in your body, whether it's positive or negative. So if you have loving feelings, they will multiply; if you feel bad, that will increase too. If this kind of exercise makes you feel irritable or upset, try putting your right hand on your groin (your base chakra, according to the Tantrics) and your left hand on your heart. This is a way of transforming negative emotions into loving ones before you continue to move your sexual energy around your body. As Mantak Chia says: 'While most men do self-pleasure, few are really able to do it lovingly, to cultivate love – make love to themselves – while they are doing it … Cultivating your sexual energy into loving-kindness will also help you not to ejaculate; it is much more difficult to maintain control when you are feeling anger or impatience.'

Think about it … isn't it harder to maintain any form of concentration, whether it's a work project or focus on a sport, when you are feeling boiled up about something? Well, the same applies to your sexual behaviour too.

THE LOCKING TECHNIQUE

Generally, Tantrics enjoy delayed ejaculation rather than semen retention. The following Tantric exercise is similar to the Taoist practice, but another summary of the process might be useful:

The next time you need to urinate, practise a few pull-ups on your PC muscle by stopping in mid-flow. Then relax the muscle and remember to use the same action when you make love. (Practise this every time you go to the loo.)

When you reach the point of 'no return' – the feeling that precipitates an ejaculatory orgasm rather than the rush of semen through the tubes – breathe in while pulling up from the perineum, and then hold the breath for a moment until the feeling has subsided.

Imagine the rush of sexual energy from your genitals being pulled up through your body. It might only get as far as your belly, but moving it is what you're after.

Try to focus on moving the energy rather than holding back the orgasm, so it's a positive action rather than a retentive one.

When your partner is nearing her own orgasm, you can make the choice to come with her or to expand your own orgasm into the full-body experience. This might take time to perfect, but keep practising.

THE PRESSURE TECHNIQUE

Pressing the Million Dollar Point (MDP) not only delays ejaculation, it can also block the semen from leaving your body once you have passed the point of no return. Using your dominant hand, press three middle fingers (with short, trimmed fingernails) into the MDP before you actually start ejaculating. This will prevent semen from leaving your prostate and entering your urethra for ejaculation. If semen does come out, it probably means that you haven't hit the MDP. Next time, try a little further down towards your anus and press harder. It is important to massage this pelvic area afterwards, to squeeze your PC muscle several times, and, ideally, to circulate your sexual energy through your body, as described above. It is also a good idea to give the area around your tail-bone a vigorous, but not brutal, rub.

MATT, 29, MUSICIAN

'I found it quite easy to learn but you get better at it, if that makes sense. It has taken me years to get really comfortable with it and to get to know my body, but it worked the first time I tried it. The basic technique is pretty simple, but you can add your own variations in terms of changing thrusting patterns as you get more used to it. I keep pushing the goalposts a bit and experimenting.'

TO THRUST OR NOT TO THRUST

The Taoists and Tantrics have a range of thrusting techniques that offer a great deal of variety beyond the quick-fire deep thrusts of the 'wham, bam, thank-you ma'am' school of limited sexual expertise. It is important to find your own rhythm according to your desires and those of your partner, but you may like to experiment with some of the techniques outlined below, if you have not tried them already.

Always make sure that your partner is fully aroused before you begin to thrust. Thrusting before she is fully lubricated and ready is a recipe for considerable discomfort on her part, an instant passion killer, which is likely to be swiftly followed by a disinclination to make love with you at all if you are not sensitive to this.

The Kama Sutra lists Nine Movements of the Man, which should be performed during lovemaking and which have charming names like The Blow of a Boar and The Sporting of a Sparrow. These are variations on how deeply a woman is penetrated and the speed or slowness required. Tantra also promotes the Thrusts of the Dragon, where the man thrusts deeply nine times and once quite shallow (three, five and seven can work well too). This can be reversed for the Thrusts of the Phoenix, when a man thrusts shallowly for nine strokes and then once very deeply. This is very powerful for the woman on the receiving end, and women who have never had a vaginal orgasm report that it is this winning combination of 'phoenix thrusts' that are the very movements that enable them to have one for the first time. If you want to be a man who drives women wild, you could do worse that use this technique – assuming, of course, that you are also lovingly connected to her on an emotional and mental level.

Emperor Huang Ti: *'And what is the method of nine shallow and one deep?'*
Su Nu: *'That means simply to thrust nine times shallow and then one deep. Each thrust should be co-ordinated with one's breathing. The depth between Lute String and Black Pearl (one to four inches) is called shallow; between Little Stream and Valley Proper (three to five inches) is called deep. Thrusting too shallowly the couple may not feel the greatest pleasure, too deeply they may be injured.'*
The Classic of the Plain Girl (translated by Jolan Chang)

The most popular thrusting method in the Taoist texts is also based on the number nine, which is associated with powerful, masculine yang energy. The rhythm is the same as for the Tantric Phoenix Thrusts, nine shallow strokes and one deep stroke. The Taoists claim it heightens pleasure, and prevents early ejaculation. This is how it should be done (accountants and men good with numbers have a distinct advantage here):

A Set of Nine consists of the following:
1   nine shallow, one deep
2   eight shallow, two deep
3   seven shallow, three deep
4   six shallow, four deep
5   five shallow, five deep
6   four shallow six deep
7   three shallow, seven deep
8   two shallow, eight deep
9   one shallow, nine deep

The aim is to go through as many Sets of Nine as possible without ejaculating. Speaking as someone who struggled through GCSE maths, I'd admire anyone who could manage that level of counting just once. As with any of these exercises, it is really the principle behind it; in other words changing the pace and speed of your thrusting to thrill your partner, which matters more than sticking exactly to the numbers proscribed. (Counting out loud isn't advisable, by the way.)

WILL, 37, WINDOW CLEANER
'I used to get really hung up on the numbers, until I realised that 36 meant 'do something a lot' and 60 meant 'do it even more'. Then I relaxed and could enjoy what I was doing rather than getting caught up in my head with whether I was at 28 or 30.'

While it may be tempting to think that a pill could sort out your sex life, the reality is that it won't help one iota if your relationship is cracked in other ways. By focusing on areas beyond the physical mechanics of sex, Tantra enables you to move beyond the idea that in order to make love satisfactorily two people need certain equipment working in one particular way and that sex is impossible without it

As well as thrusting in and out, try circling or literally 'screwing' with your hips. This way more of your partner's vagina will be stimulated, giving her an even better time. If you are not sure what to do, think Elvis Presley (so accurately nicknamed 'Elvis the Pelvis') whose hip gyrations generated sexual excitement for his screaming female fans. (I wouldn't recommend the white satin suit with the big collar, however.)

MOVING ENERGY FROM YOUR GENITALS TO YOUR BRAIN

Quite apart from all these physical techniques is the vital role that your mind will play in this. Mentally drawing energy away from your genitals and up your spine will be a big help towards preventing the ejaculatory reflex. The Taoists have a series of techniques that enable you to move energy from your genitals up to your brain, to be stored in your navel for future use.

Ever heard the expression 'navel-gazing'? This comes from the Eastern belief that the area in the body below the navel is a powerful source of energy. People who practise the martial arts use it as a focus for balance; the Taoists value it as somewhere to store the sexual energy that is generated within the body. The joy of being able to do this is that you can move your sexual energy around your body whether or not you are physically doing anything sexual at the time. So if you get unexpectedly horny at an inconvenient time, you can squeeze your PC muscle and imagine pushing the energy up your spine, into your brain and down the front of your body to your navel. Touch your tongue to the front of your palate. You may feel a light tingling along your spine and in your head as you do this. For younger guys who feel sexually aroused at awkward times this is an incredibly useful technique. No more hiding behind the newspaper on your lap on the train when a sexy thought strikes …

If you want to practise non-ejaculation seriously, the Taoist advice is that this should depend on your age, state of health and lifestyle. One recommendation is that you take your age, multiply it by 2 and then divide it by 10. So if you are 35 years old, 35 x 2 divided by 10 = 7. This is the minimum number of days you should allow between each ejaculation in order to preserve your life energy without restricting your lovemaking.

If you have ever practised meditation, yoga or any of the martial arts, you will find moving sexual energy relatively easy. If you haven't, it may take a while before you become comfortable with the idea of it. If you are experiencing problems with this, or if you are simply interested in finding out even more about sexual energy in men, I warmly recommend Mantak Chia's book, *The Multi-Orgasmic Man*, which contains many more exercises and information about the Taoist view of energy in the body.

NATALIE, 28, DESIGNER

'I had a relationship with one guy who was very keen to develop his sexual practice, but for me it just wasn't intimate enough. I didn't feel like I was really receiving anything from him. I felt like a laboratory assistant. We could have been doing exercises at Army camp. The big

difference with my present partner is that he has an entirely different attitude. And he is now very experienced at non-ejaculation; it's taken him a lot of work and I really respect that. To be blunt, I think men have to change a lot more of their sexual practice than women do, and looking back, perhaps I was too critical of my ex-partner. On the other hand, my current relationship is basically different. In the past sex has always been something that went stale or got boring. There are no signs of that and I'd say that I have finally been able to have not just fantastic sex, but sex that is meaningful, spiritual and healing. And I've never before seen a man have orgasms like my boyfriend. When we first started our relationship, I thought "I want some of that!" '

When you do get the hang of experiencing orgasm without the muscle spasm of ejaculation, you might start wondering when you should stop. The Taoists advise that you let your erection go down every 20 minutes or so, to allow the blood to recirculate throughout your body. As for stopping the sexual experience, that's up to you and your partner. Be sensitive to her/his needs as well as your own. (And don't forget that you'll still need to eat, sleep and go to work.)

The other important point is that as long as you remember to move some energy away from your genitals before you ejaculate, your body will be receiving a great deal more energy and pleasure than if you make love in the 'normal' Western way. Hold in mind that all of this is to make your life richer and more fun. If it begins to be the reverse, step back and reassess your attitude to it.

TANTRA AND THE OLDER MAN

Many men find that as they grow older their attitude to sex changes. (Women do too). Their sense of sexual urgency may wane and they find that the kind of sex they had in their twenties is no longer as satisfying as it once was. Whether or not you agree that men face a mid-life crisis at around 40, it is probably true to say that at some point around then, plenty of them start to question their priorities and sometimes their relationships.

'I was in my early thirties when I stopped experiencing the same kind of fulfilment from sex that I got in my twenties. I've noticed from my friends that it's more usual to happen at around 50. Some men panic and feel they have to find another woman in the hope that she will make them feel as sexually powerful as they did at 20. So they drop their wife, and buy a sports car or a Harley and look for a younger woman. It's a kind of desperation that drives them to seek something they think they are on the verge of losing.

What Tantra has done for me is given me an opportunity to bring a sense of balance to my sexual energy. It has changed. It's become much more a part of me and now it feels much more of a shared energy when I am with someone. It's a two-way thing and I feel a lot more able to receive from someone than I did when I was younger.'

Because Tantra offers a route away from the idea that sex is all about a man 'doing' something to a woman, it gives men the chance to move away from the feeling that the only thing in life they have to hang on to is the ability to get hard, stay hard and ejaculate.

The popularity of Viagra, the pill that promotes erections by increasing blood flow to the crotch, is a testament to the fact that men want to continue sexual activity as they grow older and their capacity to have erections may fluctuate. What is not on record, yet, is what other benefits Viagra brings to the relationship. One Italian research group found that while men who took Viagra reported increased sexual satisfaction, there wasn't a corresponding rise in satisfaction among their partners. Sex therapists believe that one of the critical factors in maintaining a woman's sexual desire is the attraction and lust that her partner feels for her. So while she may be flattered (possibly) that he wants to take Viagra to maintain his erections, if he doesn't take time to make her feel good about herself, she won't be very interested in sex.

While it may be tempting to think that a pill could sort out your sex life, the reality is that it won't help one iota if your relationship is cracked in other ways. By focusing on areas beyond the physical mechanics of sex, Tantra enables you move beyond the idea that in order to make love satisfactorily two people need certain equipment working in one particular way and that sex is impossible without it. In reality, soft penises have as many nerve endings as hard penises, and can give just as much pleasure.

Prolonged erection difficulties should always be checked out with your doctor. One possible cause may be smoking, as it causes the blood vessels and arteries to constrict. But if you only have occasional problems with your erection, then it's worth trying out the technique developed by the Taoists known as 'soft entry' (see Chapter Eight). Gently shaking, massaging and tapping your testicles daily is also a good idea to keep your sexual equipment healthy. The Taoists believe that doing this increases your production of sex hormones, relieves any pressure you may feel after lovemaking and helps circulate the blood.

SANGA, 40, MECHANIC

'In my twenties I had a strong urge to reach fulfilment in terms of ejaculation. My body felt that was what it needed – to have an emission and release stress. In my thirties that urgency changed of its own accord. I didn't experience the same kind of fulfilment as I did when I was younger. Through practising Tantra, I have learned to find sensuousness in place of sexual gratification and pursuit. It has given me an opportunity to balance my sexual energy, so that it is now something that is much more part of me. Tantra has offered me a route to feeling whole again.'

5

TANTRA AND THE ART OF BEING SINGLE

Bookstore shelves in the West are lined with advice on how to meet the right partner. There are tips on what to wear; what to talk about; even how long to hold someone's gaze if you are interested in them (between three and four seconds direct eye contact focusing on their left eye, incidentally). Some lay out rigid rules for women about the 'right' way to make a man want to marry them; others tell men to shave off their beards, take up cookery classes and act assertively around women (though not, presumably, all at the same time). At best they give useful guidance on dating for people who are shy or out of practice. At worst they suggest that manipulating other people's thoughts and feelings, in the same way as an angler might reel in a reluctant fish, is a perfectly acceptable way to behave.

No matter how doubtful their maxims might seem, these books sell because society places value on couples. Most of our films and fairytales end with weddings or the triumph of so-called 'true love'. Equally, people who don't have partners can be made to feel like second-class citizens, or as if they are lacking in some vital way.

But from Romeo and Juliet to the young lovers in TV soaps, the kind of passion portrayed in Western films and literature rarely leads to happy endings in real life. More usually, it echoes a pattern in which one person feels they are made whole solely by the existence of another. As a result people start making declarations such as, 'I can't live without you' or 'No one has ever made me feel the way you do'. While these feelings seem real enough to the person who is experiencing them at the time, they are actually based on a false premise – namely the notion that we gain our sense of wholeness, or even happiness, from someone else, and this other person alone has the power to make us feel either terrific or terrible. This isn't true. But either knowingly or unknowingly, we grant our partners this power (perhaps because of those role models we have seen on TV and read about in books), and it's then that our relationships, which are based on a reliance on our partners to bring us happiness, begin to fray at the edges or eventually disintegrate.

Tantra offers a different perspective both on relationships and on being single. Tantra emphasises each individual's wholeness and perfection, which is something that you experience through your true self. In other words, you don't need another person to fill up your life. Of course, we can have wonderful relationships and grow through our relationships with others. But we do not need a partner to provide our happiness. Our joy in life lies within. Tantra enables you to locate the source of this joy and, as a result, to become more loving and more alive, without relying on another person to make you feel good.

SEXUALITY AND BEING SINGLE

Tantra is especially relevant to single people, because it acknowledges that we all have sexual energy, whether we are in a sexual relationship with anyone else or not. Our sexual energy is involved in the whole of life. According to Tantra teacher John: 'Tantra teaches you how to be in your aliveness, how to enjoy your erotic energy without having to go to bed with someone. That can be very liberating.'

Accepting that you can be sexy and can enjoy sexual energy without necessarily having a sexual relationship is a new idea in the West. But by acknowledging that sexual energy exists in all of us, no matter what our age, sexual orientation or marital status, Tantra allows us to access this powerful energy and enjoy it fully. According to Tantra teacher Leora: 'Tantra is about our own sexual energy as much as it is about our energy in connection with a partner. And particularly for a single person who is not physically having sex with anyone, you need to look at how you are using your sexual energy. Tantra can help you feel better about yourself and use your sexual energy more creatively. You can develop a sense of expansion and increase your vitality.'

Most people tend to shut down on their sexual energy if they are not with a partner. Sometimes this leads to frustration; more often it means they are missing out on a vital part of themselves. Practising some of the exercises outlined below can change your attitude to your sexuality. Once you have accepted that you don't need another person around for you to enjoy your sexual energy fully, you're halfway there.

WALK WITH AN AWARENESS OF YOUR PELVIS

Ever heard the expression 'strut your stuff'? There is a Tantric equivalent to this. You don't have to go as far as wiggling your bottom, but you can try walking and noticing your pelvic area and how that feels as you walk.

Some film stars and models have this down to a fine art. They radiate sexual energy from their hips as they move. Think of John Travolta walking (or strutting) down the street at the beginning of the movie *Saturday Night Fever* (it's worth getting a copy of the video just to see his walk) or the even more famous Marilyn Monroe wiggle in practically every movie she ever made. You don't have to walk in a way that will deliberately attract sexual attention from others. But it might be a novelty worth exploring to walk in a way that makes you aware of your own sexual energy instead of plodding around feeling as heavy as a sack of potatoes (as most of us do for most of the time) – and about as attractive ...

CONNECT WITH YOUR OWN SEXUAL ENERGY

Remember, harnessing sexual energy does not need to involve another person. In Tantra people learn how to transform masturbation into self-pleasuring. This turns a process that many people think of as a sexual 'quick-fix' into a way of honouring and loving yourself.

Follow the routine below to get in touch with your own sexual energy:

1   Set aside some time to give yourself the same attention that you would devote to a lover.

2   Create a warm, pleasant environment. Again, imagine that you are preparing for a lover to visit you. Make the same amount of effort. Tidy away the debris from the room you plan to use, dim the lights, put on a favourite CD (if it's Papa Roach swap it for something slightly more soothing) and light a candle or two.

3   Start by touching and feeling your whole body, as if for the first time. Some people like to anoint themselves with massage oil; others prefer something less slippery such as body lotion.

4   Think about the way you touch yourself. Often we touch ourselves in a way that we would hate to be touched by anyone else. Try to bring love into your hands and stroke your body all over before you concentrate on your genitals.

5   When you begin to pleasure yourself, try to stay as relaxed as you can, instead of tensing your thighs or belly. Imagine breathing into those areas instead of tensing.

Very few people admire themselves, enjoy their own company and treat their minds and bodies with respect. If they did, why would so many of us moan about our looks; seek one-night stands in order not to be alone; watch mindless films and TV; eat junk food or smoke cigarettes?

6   Place your other hand on your heart. Or try taking the energy up to your
    'third eye' (see page 23) and touching the point in your forehead between your
    eyebrows. This may result in your seeing images of light or brightness if you
    close your eyes.

7   When you are feeling quite aroused, take plenty of time to relax instead of
    feeling the need to speed up towards orgasm. Always remember, move down
    a gear instead of up.

8   In many instances, masturbation tends to be a way of finding a release instead
    of enjoying the process. When you move to self-pleasuring, pay special
    attention to your body, rather than completely losing yourself in the rush
    towards orgasm.

9   Don't slip into a sexual fantasy, but be present with yourself instead. This is a
    big change for most people as it involves being aware of your mind and body
    at the same time. Some people fear that they won't become aroused without
    a fantasy, but it is perfectly possible to manage without one. As Tantra teacher
    Leora explains,

'There is a world of difference between the experience of loving yourself and
losing yourself in a sexual fantasy. It is not that enjoying a fantasy is bad, but it is a
very different experience to be really present with yourself and your body instead.'

This exercise may not be as easy as you might expect. Most of us have surprising
barriers to loving ourselves in this way, but it is worth experimenting with it and
moving over any hurdles your unconscious mind may set up for you. If you find it
tough to begin with, simply notice what thoughts come up and then let them go
without getting caught in a mire of negative judgements and analysis. Try again
with the attitude that you are doing something beneficial for yourself and see
where it takes you.

    If you find this exercise rather too challenging (and you are meant to be
enjoying yourself, after all), concentrate on the Heaven and Earth meditation (see
page 208) – also when you are feeling comfortable, in warm, pleasant surroundings.

'For me the process of turning masturbation into self-pleasuring is like charging up a battery that is your sexual energy. Once you are charged up in that respect you can use that energy for other things, whether it's work or meditation.'

KUNDALINI SHAKING

A good way of getting in touch with your sexual energy by yourself is to practise Kundalini shaking. This sounds like an African ritual, and is not a million miles away from the sort of rhythmic tribal dancing that you might find in an African village or even on the London club scene.

Kundalini is Sanskrit for 'coiled up', and it refers to the energy that is stored in the base of the spine. In Tantric images, it's depicted as a sleeping serpent, which lies coiled three-and-a-half times. The snake has long been linked with sexuality (think of Adam and Eve in the Garden of Eden), but the associations it has in Tantra are rather more positive.

There is a branch of yoga dedicated to releasing this energy, but it can also be stirred by music, dance and making love (see page 28). If you want a taste of how this energy feels, try the following exercise, which is known as Kundalini shaking:

Put on some fast dance music and turn up the volume so that it's loud enough for you to focus on the beat (but not so loud the police turn up). Close your eyes. Stand with your spine straight, with your arms relaxed and your knees bent. Bending your knees stresses the thighs and calves, which will produce tiny tremors after a few minutes. Imagine yourself on a platform that is moving underneath your feet and that you are trying to keep your balance. Rock very gently, and sense the trembling that is building up in your legs. Don't try and control it. If you feel uncomfortable, shift your position. Allow the tremors to move up into your body and into your abdomen.

When you feel ready, lie down on some cushions or a mattress and picture the energy rising up through your body to the top of your head. This may be a very gentle process, or you may shake quite profoundly. Don't be alarmed if you do. Just concentrate on moving the energy upwards until the shaking slowly dies away. Afterwards, you should be left with a feeling of peace and relaxation. You may feel slightly (but pleasantly) light-headed. Lie back and enjoy it.

START A LOVE AFFAIR WITH YOURSELF

You can begin a love affair with yourself. This is not as strange as it may sound at first. It is about being open to finding pleasure and enjoyment and a sense of completeness in yourself that you may or may not choose to share with another individual. Ironically, if you enjoy a love affair with yourself, you will not only be better equipped to tackle life on your own, but will also be more likely to attract a partner (if you that's what you want) and to bring richer and deeper qualities to any future relationship.

So how do you do it? When people begin a good relationship with someone else, they do everything in their power to bring happiness to their beloved. They admire their lover's qualities, enjoy their company and treat them with respect. How many times have you heard people looking back with fondness on how special their partner made them feel in the early days?

There are few things in life more pleasurable than being the focus of someone's love, and receiving big chunks of tenderness, approval and admiration. Bearing in mind that you are the source of your own joy, you don't have to be Einstein to appreciate that this behaviour, which you normally reserve for other people, can be translated into caring for yourself. It sounds simple and straightforward, yet very few people admire themselves, enjoy their own company and treat their minds and bodies with respect. If they did, why would so many of us moan about our looks; seek one-night stands in order not to be alone; watch mindless films and TV; eat junk food or smoke cigarettes?

Beginning a love affair with yourself marks the start of a new relationship with your mind and body. It is about acceptance, integrity, mental stimulation and nourishment. If you're in doubt about how to make it work, just ask yourself, Am I doing something I would recommend or want to share with someone I really loved? It's pretty much a failsafe test. Take exercise, for example. Yes, you'd probably want a partner to look after their body and do the best they could to stay healthy for as long as possible. So why shouldn't you want the same for yourself?

Or take smoking. Do you really want to be around someone who's wreathed in cigarette smoke and tastes like an old ash-tray? If the answer is No, is it really such a good idea to carry on smoking yourself? The same applies to following a healthy diet and stimulating an inquiring mind. Think of the admirable physical and mental qualities you'd seek in a partner and ask yourself if you share them. And if you don't, work out how you can. If 'loving yourself more' sounds a bit too vague, work out the practical steps you can take so you can match your ideal partner.

EVE, 54, NURSING MANAGER

'When my last long-term relationship ended, I decided that I would like to meet a life partner. Not necessarily to get married, but someone with whom I could have a lifelong commitment. I thought about going to dating agencies or getting all my friends to matchmake for me, and I suppose one day I might do that. But first, I've decided to work on myself. I thought, if I can do things that will make me a higher quality individual, then it's more likely that I will attract someone that I will find admirable. It's an upside down way to the way most people go about trying to find relationships; in the past I've always looked for someone who would make me feel better. Now I want someone who will make me feel good, of course, but I'll be confident and happy in my own right first.'

If all this sounds a bit too worthy, remember one crucial ingredient for loving yourself more. Always be open to having fun. Laughter, after all, is a powerful tool for healing. Even Western medicine has now accepted that the endorphins (or the so-called 'feel-good hormones') released when we have a really good laugh are good for our physical and mental wellbeing.

BERNADETTE, 31, TEACHER

'I feel I have got more self love through practising Tantra and somehow more integrity. Tantra has given me an inner confidence. It has made me so self sufficient, and so able to meet my

own sexual needs that I didn't worry about being on my own or needing to meet a partner. At one point, I remember thinking that I was having such a great time on my own that it would be hard work to fit someone else into my life. In fact, I am in a committed relationship now and I'm really happy, but if I found I was on my own again in the future, it wouldn't panic me at all. I also think it's important to practise some of the Tantric exercises on your own, to maintain that sense of your whole self.'

IF YOU ARE LOOKING FOR A RELATIONSHIP ...

Not everyone is single by choice. If you would like a partner and haven't yet found the right person, it's worth examining the beliefs you have about yourself, your body and your sexuality. Tantra helps you do this. According to Tantra teacher Leora:

'Your beliefs about yourself are integral in terms of who you will attract, if anyone. If you are walking around thinking "I am an unattractive failure", it's unlikely that loads of people are going to rush to fall in love with you, even if you are beautiful and interesting. With such a negative attitude, you won't let anyone else in.

Self-esteem, as it's commonly known, is highly important and any kind of therapeutic work should help you. Tantra workshops help you to look at how these kind of beliefs arise, usually they stem from previous relationships with others, whether these are family or romantic relationships. In my opinion they are best healed with other people, so doing a workshop with other single people, or exploring it in another therapeutic way, is very important. There is a limit to what we can embark on without that kind of support.'

Any kind of personal development work, whether it is attending a Tantra workshop, learning to play an instrument or taking up quilting, is a good place to begin if you would like to attract a partner. Traditional books on dating advocate these things as practical ways of meeting someone new, and to an extent they are right; widening your social circle by going on personal development courses or

taking up new hobbies will ensure that you meet more people.

My suggestion, though, is that you do this for yourself, and that you regard meeting others as secondary to the fun and enjoyment that your new hobby will bring you. Stiff-jawed partner-hunters have a look of desperation in their eyes and usually attract only the equally desperate. Happy, fulfilled people, on the other hand, attract others without any effort on their part. Work toward the goal of finding fun and joy for yourself and you'll be tripping over people who want to get to know you.

PRIYATAMA, 52, SEX THERAPIST

'I wasn't in a relationship when I first became interested in Tantra, so I went on a couple of workshops and had a lot of fun within a very safe environment. I learned about saying "Yes" and "No" and what my boundaries were in terms of how sensual I wanted to be with someone that I wasn't in a relationship with.

After about two years I went into a relationship, and I remember saying, "I don't know how to do sex any more" because my attitudes towards my sexuality had changed so much. I had learnt to differentiate between the casual sexual connection I might have made before and the deeper, more honouring connection that I knew I wanted in future. And I wasn't going to settle for less. And I haven't. My new partner didn't have to know everything about Tantra, but he did need to be willing to explore it with me, and travel together in that way. And that's what we've been doing ever since.'

Nearly all of the single people I interviewed about Tantra had attended Tantra workshops by themselves. Virtually all of them said they were apprehensive beforehand. They shared varying degrees of nervousness, from slight misgivings to serious panic, but every one said they had found them useful and enjoyable experiences.

CATHERINE, 33, OCCUPATIONAL THERAPIST

'My friends had some of the preconceived ideas that people have about Tantra – that a workshop will be a kinky mass orgy – and I did worry that I might be getting into *something alone that I couldn't control. But as soon as the teacher said at the beginning that no one was under any pressure to do anything they were not comfortable with, I decided that I was safe to stay.*

I was very happy with the people I landed up working with. And the exercises were interesting, but not terribly intimate. I had my personal boundaries before the course began and I stuck with them. I knew that no matter what, I wouldn't be taking my clothes off!'

SANGA, 40, MECHANIC

'I found attending Tantra workshops on my own really liberating. I feel that if I'd had a partner there, I would have had to look out for them as well as me, and it felt good just to be able to focus on myself and what I was getting out of it.'

RACHEL, 34, LECTURER

'I've been on Tantra courses with a partner and as a single person, and I have to say I had a better time when I was single! When I was with my partner, we'd have relationship stuff come up and that would get in the way of what we were doing, whereas if you do it on your own, you are really just working on yourself.'

BERNADETTE, 31, TEACHER

'I think there are good things on both sides. When you work with a partner in Tantra there are two energy fields to contend with, when you are on your own, it's clearer what's going on. On the other hand, when you are working with someone else you are generating a lot more energy, so in my experience it's been easier to reach a higher level of ecstasy with a partner.'

David and Ellen Ramsdale, in their book *Sexual Energy Ecstasy*, have written a poem called 'Happiness is knowing you are single', which sums up what this chapter is about:

Alone forever
Are you

Whether your consorts are none, one,
few or many
They have but one face

A reflection in the mirror

Those who are joined
Will eventually part

Those who are a part
Will eventually be whole

All is a process of
Uniting and separating

Do not be fooled by appearances

How can relationships be permanent
When life itself is not?

No one can love you
Unless you love you

The greatest love, the sweetest love, the
best love
Stands on ground sanctified
By a love of freedom

Without fresh air
Even the finest fire
Dies

6

GETTING INTO
THE MOOD

There is a saying, 'Men want sex, women want romance', which sums up our upside-down, modern view of sex. It implies, first, that women don't want sex, and second that men don't want romance. Neither of which is true.

Admittedly, there are some men who are irked by the thought they might have to buy their girlfriend dinner, jewellery, or at least take her to the cinema, in order to have sex with her. These sad souls are confusing romance with prostitution. And there may be women who believe that in order to feel desirable, they need a man to spend large amounts of cash on them. They are making the same mistake.

Should you feel any of these things, the chances are that you have been hypnotized by advertising. Most ads, which are, of course, trying to sell as many products as they can, suggest that caring about someone inevitably involves some sort of financial transaction. It doesn't. Tantric sex is about being prepared to give to your partner first, but this doesn't mean that your gifts must be material ones.

It could be giving your time, attention or ability to listen, or fixing a cupboard, that will lead to your partner wanting to relate to you in a more sexual way. Interestingly, studies have shown that men who help around the house have sex with their partners more often than those who don't. This suggests that flashing a bottle of Ajax, rather than flashing your credit cards or stuffing your pockets with Viagra, is one of the best keys to an improved sex life. In the West we have grown accustomed to the 'Me first' attitude. So if you are a man who turns to his wife in bed after she has spent a day working, shopping, and getting the kids to do their homework and whispers 'Fancy a shag?' don't be surprised if you are not met with an entirely enthusiastic response.

If, on the other hand, you have offered to go to the supermarket and helped cook dinner, or even told her to put her feet up with a glass of wine while you wash up, you may be pleasantly surprised by a tap on the shoulder and a passionate kiss later in the evening. And this is not about trading domestic tasks, instead of money, for sex. Demonstrating that you care for your partner and that you want to take care of him or her is a significantly different approach.

Equally, there's nothing wrong with buying gifts when the occasion feels right. It comes down to your intention behind them. And when you are both prepared to 'give first' you will be amazed by the loving feelings this will generate.

How much pleasure can I give my partner?

A Tantric approach to sex does not have to be especially time-consuming, although if you can allow a couple of hours together, so much the better. Just deciding on an early night can be enough if you are both hard-pressed for time. The most important aspect is to begin your sexual encounter with a changed attitude, which can be briefly summed up as 'How much love and pleasure can I give my partner?'

The title of this chapter is 'Getting into the Mood' because Tantra acknowledges that few of us can slip into a state of sexual arousal instantaneously. And if we do, it is more likely to lead to a quickie than anything else. While this may be an attractive enough option on a menu, if that's really all you sex life adds up to, it's rather like eating the same meal every day; and human beings need a degree of variety to keep their interest and enthusiasm alive in almost anything, including food and sex.

While men may, as a rule, become turned on more quickly than women, if they want their partners to really enjoy their lovemaking, (and, to be fair to most men, they invariably do), they understand that taking time to treat sex as something involving intimacy and pleasure – and not just a brief peak of excitement – is a worthwhile thing to do.

The following pages offer some suggestions on preparing yourself, mentally and physically, for Tantric sex. Some of it may cover familiar territory; some of the ideas may be new. As ever, if trying to incorporate it all into your routine feels a bit daunting, try just one or two options and get the hang of those before you move on to experiment with other new experiences.

Hygiene

Never expect a partner to cover you in kisses if you don't smell good. Don't ask your partner if they would like you to shower or brush your teeth before you make love with them – do it anyway. There are, of course, fashions in hygiene like everything else. (In the 18th century, the Emperor Napoleon wrote to Josephine, 'Home in five days – don't wash.') The French have a word, cassolette, for the intimate scent of a woman. Some men adore it (depending on the woman), others don't. My suggestion is to err on the side of cleanliness. It's more acceptable (and less upsetting) to be urged by a lover not to wash than the other way around.

SOME IMPORTANT INFORMATION FOR MEN

Quite apart from the obvious fact that no one likes to be near men who smell unpleasant, a lot of women equate a man being careful about his personal cleanliness with an emotional safety net. In other words, if a man bothers about making himself clean and fresh, then he is bothering about her. However, if he climbs into bed still sweating from the office and the journey home, and emitting a lingering aroma of beer and cigarettes, she won't feel taken care of, and most women's initial instinct is to slide away to the opposite side of the bed and pretend to be asleep.

SMELL IGNITES SEXUAL ENERGY

In Tantric teaching, our sense of smell can ignite our sexual energy. Smell also affects our emotional reactions more than any other sense and can alter our energy level too. One of the reasons for this is that scent detected by the olfactory nerve makes an impact on the brain immediately, while food and drink have to enter the bloodstream before the body can react to them fully. In Greece, more than 2000 years ago, the father of modern medicine, Hippocrates, recommended the benefits of aromatics. The Bible also refers to healing with aromatic oils. Before Biblical times, people believed that scenting a room with rare and special fragrances would attract gods and angels and at the same time repel negative forces. Stirring our sense of smell is too important to get wrong.

PERFUME

While an unpleasant whiff is a turn-off, the positive smell of perfumes or essential oils on clean skin, can have a powerful effect in making us feel aroused. Our smell receptors are so sensitive that a single molecule of some substances is enough to stimulate one receptor ending. Research has shown that our olfactory organs can sense less than one hundred millionth of a gram of musk. When you are choosing a

Never expect a partner

to cover you in kisses if

you don't smell

good. **Don't ask** your

partner if they would

like you to shower

or brush your

teeth before you

make love with them –

do it anyway

perfume or aftershave, bear in mind that less is more – an occasional waft of a fabulous smell is preferable to drowning in it.

Everyone has their own PH balance, which is the skin's acidity/alkaline ratio, and this will vary according to mood and body temperature. A smoker's skin, for example, will not hold perfume for as long as a non-smoker's; dry skin will allow perfume to evaporate faster than oily skin; sweat will wash away perfume. Hot, muggy weather will increase the impact of your scent far more than cool, dry weather.

When choosing a new perfume, dab it on your skin and wait at least 10 minutes for your own skin chemicals to react with the scent. This can be tricky when you are being pursued by a woman behind a beauty counter in a department store who offers a squirt of spray and waits for an instant reaction to know if you want to buy. Go and have a coffee while you wait for the perfume to adjust to your body. What may have smelt divine on your best friend could prove a hellish pong on you.

If you are someone who tries to eke out the very last drops of your favourite scent over months and years, beware. Time, as well as extreme heat and cold, can destroy the delicate balance of oils, fixative and alcohol that make up its unique fragrance.

ESSENTIAL OILS

Choose good-quality essential oils (rather than their cheaper chemical counterparts) and store them in a cool place, away from sunlight. Essential oils are, as their name implies, essences distilled from a huge range of natural sources, such as flowers, herbs, fruits, the bark of trees and herbs. Never underestimate their power; always read the instructions on labels or consult a qualified aromatherapist if you need advice. Never apply them directly on to the skin, but dilute them according to their instructions with a natural vegetable oil, such as grapeseed, sunflower or almond. Don't use more than three at any one time or your sense of smell will be overwhelmed.

Certain essential oils have gained a reputation over the centuries for enhancing lovemaking. Sandalwood has a sensual impact on the body and a calming effect on the mind. Jasmine is associated with male sexuality and rose with femininity. Ylang-ylang is usually promoted for its erotic powers, although I have to confess that I can't stand the smell of it. (A note of caution here. Essential oils are great but they don't have universal appeal. If you prefer to fill your special space with a quick squirt of Chanel No. 5 or even a few drops of Brut, as long as both of you love the smell, that's perfectly OK.)

BERNADETTE, 31, TEACHER

'More thought goes into the way I arrange my bedroom when I have sex with my partner now. I think about the music I'm going to put on, I use essential oils and alter the lighting. It is great fun setting it up, and the result is that I feel more relaxed and I'm able to be more receptive to the whole experience. Making an effort with the room helps to get me into the right frame of mind.'

THE PERFECT SETTING

If you think of sex as a gift, then the wrapping makes all the difference. It may be a truism to say that your environment influences your mood, but it is astonishing how many people ignore this when it comes to making love with their partner.

In the early days of sexual excitement, when simply being touched by your lover is powerfully intoxicating, you can make love in the most unappealing surroundings – an aircraft toilet, the back seat of a car, a motorway service station – and it doesn't matter. It may even boost the excitement you feel when you're together. As time goes on your love may grow, but the chemical rush you get simply from brushing against your partner wanes. This is the time to pay attention to when and where you make love.

Conventional sex therapists usually suggest making love in different rooms of the house or booking a weekend away in a hotel without the children to perk up your love life. While this may work for a while, it may not make practical or financial sense to you. If you have no money for a weekend away and your bedroom is the only private space in your home, your options are limited. Also, it doesn't address the heart of what is going on between you.

A man can whisk his partner away from the family to an expensive hotel and be disappointed when she takes the opportunity to fall fast asleep the minute her head hits the plump pillows on the four-poster bed. Simply relocating may not be enough to rekindle the fire that once existed between you. It may be necessary to change your attitude to the way you make love first. Tantra enables you to do this.

Tantrics create a 'sacred space' for their lovemaking. They hold on to the idea that if you are going to treat your partner as a divine reflection of yourself, then it is only right to ensure that the place in which you make love with them is as pleasing as possible to both of you. This doesn't mean that you have to spend hours completing a complicated make-over on your bedroom to turn it into an exotic boudoir. But certain preparations, however minimal, to create a 'nest', or at least somewhere you feel warm and relaxed with your partner, are invaluable and can make a profound difference to your sexual experience.

After all, mood is altered, either consciously or unconsciously, by surroundings. One study of 2000 visitors to art galleries in spring 2001 by the Institute of Psychoanalytical Psychiatry in Rome showed that a visit to an art museum, or even a church 'stimulates the erotic senses'. At least a fifth of those interviewed had been so excited by what they saw that they either had a 'fleeting but intense erotic adventure' with someone they had not met before, or, if already accompanied, had experienced an 'amorous upsurge' involving 'unexpected experimentation'.

Art galleries have long been established as good venues to meet potential partners; while you are admiring a painting on a wall, you back away for a better perspective and, oops, you bump into someone who already shares one of your interests. But according to the Italian report, it wasn't just the opportunity of meeting a fellow art lover that appealed to the visitors. It was the excitement of being surrounded by the stirring beauty of the works of art themselves that awakened sexual excitement in the onlookers.

The artist most guaranteed to set pulses racing, by the way, was Gianlorenzo Bernini, whose sculptures of Pluto and Persephone in the Villa Borghese – in which the god of the underworld, Pluto, carries off his bride in manly triumph – was rated as one of the most erotic art works in Rome. Some visitors to the church of Santa Maria della Vittoria in the same city claim to have been stirred by Bernini's The Ecstasy of St Teresa, which ostensibly depicts the saint's spiritual transports. Apparently, in the 18th century the sight of the saint with her head thrown back and eyes half-closed led the French scholar Charles de Brosses to comment: 'If that is divine love, then I know what it is.' Perhaps Bernini (and other artists) instinctively knew more about Tantric principles than we assume.

Lighting

Every magazine in your newsagent advises you to light candles when you want to relax or create a mellow ambience – with good reason. Candles calm the spirit and can heighten the erotic experience. They create a soft, skin-caressing light that makes the human shape look fluid and smooth. By way of contrast, the average household electric light bulb sends out a pallid yellow light with a dash of orange in it. The overall effect of this on the human body is to tinge the flesh with grey, white and yellow tones that are, at the very least, extremely unflattering. Bearing in mind that the brain gets 75 per cent of its sensory information through the eyes, a change in the way you light your bedroom may result in an improvement in your love life.

I recommend red and pink candles for practising Tantra (for me the colours signify passion and love) but there are others who swear by coloured bulbs. Cool tones such as green and blue are meant to be erotically effective; red isn't advisable because it is considered over-stimulating. Fans of coloured bulbs point to the psychological illusions created by coloured lighting. In one US study, men under blue and green lighting reported that their partner's breasts not only looked larger, but felt larger when touched (I can't work out the science on that one). Under the same lighting, women saw men's penises as larger than life (though I wouldn't recommend men carry a torch with a green or blue bulb on dates). Tests on college students revealed that red illumination hastened erection while green illumination slowed it down – a possible explanation of why prostitutes favour red lights.

Whether or not you want to go to the trouble of changing the bulbs in your light fittings, accepting that lighting plays an important role in changing your mood is an important first step in creating a special space for you and your partner.

JAMES, 45, ELECTRICIAN

'I think it's important to create a special atmosphere. When you first fall in love with someone, you can have the special atmosphere anywhere, whether it's on the bus or in a fish and chip shop. When you are more familiar with them, you have to create it consciously. One way of achieving it is to light candles and make the place in which you make love special. But you have to be careful not to get too caught up in it and think that's all you have to do. So I think of it as a tool to be used and that's all. It's actually about creating a special atmosphere between you and your partner. Having a nice room can help, but it doesn't end there.'

THE BEDROOM

Most people opt to create a special space for Tantra in their bedroom, as it's the most private place in their home. Here are a couple of basic suggestions that will help. Firstly, clear out the clutter and anything related to work. Piles of ironing, heaps of shoes and dirty laundry should be tidied away as you clean the room, wipe the windows and sweep the floor. Secondly, pay special attention to the far right-hand corner of the room as you stand with the door behind you.

According to the ancient Chinese art of Feng Shui, just as we have an energy body overlaying the physical body called the meridian system (which is used in acupuncture and all other forms of Chinese medicine), so your home is overlapped by an energy grid system called the Bagua. This reflects various aspects of your life, as the energy in your home is not separate from the energy in you and in the world around you. The far right-hand corner of each room is your relationship corner, and if all you have in it is a chipped coffee mug and an old slipper, then your partnership may not be in its best possible state.

Choose your colours carefully ...

Everyone responds to colour slightly differently; one man's chocolate brown may be another woman's muddy sludge. Memories, too, may cloud our appreciation of colour. How many items of clothing do you now own that are the same colour as your school uniform? On the other hand, there are some underlying effects associated with colour that it may be useful to bear in mind. The following list links a colour to the emotions it is said to stimulate:

- Blue: peace, trust, calm
  - Brown: stability, reliability, groundedness
  - Green: growth, vitality, life, abundance
  - Lavender: fantasy, romance, imagination
  - Pink: commitment, compassion, companionship
- Purple: passion, inner vision, spirituality
- Red: pleasure, vigour, persistence
  - Teal: creativity, energy, serenity
    - Yellow: playfulness, eagerness, confidence

Altars

As the human psyche responds to symbols, some people choose to create a small altar in their bedroom that reflects their feelings for each other and contains symbols of the wider world as well. Altars are not only found in churches. The dictionary definition of an altar is a 'flat topped block for offerings to a deity' but this is rather narrow. The word is derived from the Latin meaning 'high place' and history reveals that people have wanted to create altars from the earliest times. Neanderthal people in caves high up in the Alps celebrated the Paleolithic cult of the bear, which was associated with motherhood, 75,000 years ago, and altars have been found in the Egyptian pyramids and in dozens of other ancient cultures.

At their simplest level altars are arrangements of physical objects that have a wider meaning, whether this reflects an ideal, a belief, a relationship or an idea. These individual tokens become part of a bigger picture and their power lies in what they represent to the human mind.

Not everyone feels comfortable with the idea of having an altar in their home. This is possibly because so many people associate them with churches and the Christian religion and feel uneasy with the idea of any form of religious ritual behind their own front door. A Tantric altar should be free of all of these associations

If making an altar to celebrate your partnership sounds rather grand, or even ungodly, remember, all that you are doing is consciously gathering items together that have meaning for you both, in the same way as you might carefully arrange a group of photographs or the objects on the mantelpiece above your fire.

In her book, *Altars*, the writer Denise Linn suggests that you remind yourself that true love is really a deepening of the connection between yourself, others and the Divine, or whatever represents the Divine in your life. Linn recommends covering a surface with a soft velvet or gauze fabric in red or purple, placing rose quartz and fresh flowers on it with pink candles and a pair of objects, including photographs. She also says that your altar should contain something to remind you of what divine love means to you.

The size of the altar is not important. Move the objects on it around and place new ones there from time to time. Don't become too possessive about it. Occasionally give away items from your altar, although if it is a love altar that contains things that are important to both of you, it might be wise to ask your partner's permission first ...

RACHEL, 34, LECTURER

'My boyfriend and I created a little love temple, we put crystals and candles and a Buddha on it and it made a huge difference to me because it was as if we were both saying, "This is something special". It felt like we were valuing our relationship, and it was so different from having sex when you are tired and falling into bed at 11p.m. a bit drunk. It made us very close. And we shared a lot of affection and tenderness as a result.'

Not everyone feels comfortable with the idea of having an altar in their home. This is possibly because so many people associate them with churches and the Christian religion and feel uneasy with the idea of any form of religious ritual behind their own front door. A Tantric altar should be free of all of these associations. You won't be worshipping the items on your altar. It is simply a reminder of love in the middle of everyday life.

WAYNE, 34, ANTIQUES RESTORER
'Altars don't do anything for me because I feel my altar is inside my head. My idea of a special space to make love is outdoors at night, under the stars in a field. What could be more sacred than to be in the thick of nature? Having said that, as long as you can have some space where you won't be interrupted and somewhere you feel comfortable, then that is enough for me. But everyone is different. Some people say that they get a lot of energy from having an altar near them.'

FOOD

Avoid making love immediately after a big meal. Your body needs to focus on digesting. Taoists recommend that when you've eaten you should feel satisfied, not stuffed. This is because as the food settles in your stomach you will become full. They say the same applies to sex. When you finish lovemaking, you should also be satisfied, but have a little desire left over. Then, as your energy settles, you will become content.

Lots of people share food as a prelude to making love, and this can be a pleasurable way of engaging the senses. If you plan to visit a restaurant, choose food that will not leave you bloated and unable to move afterwards; otherwise the last thing you will feel like doing is anything sexual. A light meal beforehand, or some exotic fruit and a glass of wine shared in your Tantric space, is ideal.

CLOTHES

A personal confession here. I was thrilled to discover that Tantra encourages women to dress up and wear make-up. (I'm relieved I never had a calling to be a nun; a wimple and no Christian Dior lipstick would have been the toughest spiritual path for me.) Tantra is about celebrating your love and the love of the Divine and women are encouraged to dress as though they were goddesses.

Like the concept of creating an altar, this is something that will appeal more to some than others. It is certainly not compulsory to do anything in Tantra, and if you are a woman and the idea of wearing make-up or sensual clothes leaves you cold, then it doesn't mean that Tantra is not for you. It's the intention behind the action that matters, so if you can feel completely gorgeous without a smudge of eyeshadow and a stitch of clothing, then that's fine too.

While researching Tantra, I came across an Indian book that I thought – being physically and culturally closer to the original source – would concentrate purely on its spiritual and ascetic aspects. I couldn't have been more wrong. A small paperback, first published in Bombay in 1976 and reprinted annually, judging by the cover, it contains an entire chapter on erotic dress. Although the book points out that this wasn't part of original Tantric practice, it stresses that changes in male and female appearance satisfy the modern mind and that full nudity itself can be surprisingly unerotic.

'Subtle concealment is erotic, dressing out of context is erotic, nudity in an unusual setting is erotic,' according to Arvind and Shanta Kale, the authors of *Tantra: The Secret Power of Sex*. For women they list a surprisingly lengthy number of erotic garments, including those we are familiar with in the West, such as stockings and suspenders; high heels; leather skirts; G-strings; and crotchless knickers.

The Indian perspective on sexy clothes, though, is somehow more imaginative (and more elegant) … Hats and dark glasses worn with nothing else sound like they could provide a few laughs if not instant passion; they also suggest silky harem trousers and a brief waistcoat; a gypsy-style skirt and see-through blouse; and a sari draped sheath-like across the front of the body and then over the shoulder. The Kales advise: 'It should, however, be worn without a bra or blouse so that the movements of the naked breasts under the single fold of the sheer material are clearly visible.' Jewellery, they point out, gives a woman an especially sexy glow

If you want your sex life to stay exactly as it is, keep on doing what you are doing. If, on the other hand, you would like it to move forward to a higher plane of enjoyment and satisfaction, be prepared to try something different, even if you do have initial reservations when it adorns her naked body. Rings, bangles and necklaces draw attention to slim fingers, shapely arms and soft breasts.

My favourite suggestion (though not one I've tried, I admit) is their recommendation to:

'...take a tip from the attractive Naga women and cover your body in beads: and very little else ... The more colourful the beads are the better but make sure that they are not too heavy to be worn and that they have been strongly strung. It might be worth your while to have them re-strung on strong nylon fishing line or, if you have the time, to do the stringing yourself. The anticipation of the use to which they are going to be put will make your task a light one; it will also maintain your sexual tension throughout the day, a very useful discipline for a Tantrist. Remember, however, that the beads should be long enough to cover you from neck to thigh and that there should be no need to wear anything underneath them.'

The Kales also turn their attention to men. They lament the lack of variety a man has to choose from, but mention that the Romantic Poet look – tight trousers and baggy white shirt open to the waist – still appeals to a lot of women. (The sight of similarly attired British actor Colin Firth emerging from a swim in a lake in the role of Mr Darcy in BBC TV's adaptation of *Pride and Prejudice* filled millions of sofa-bound women with rampant desire ...)

Although the Kales finally decide on well-fitting swimming trunks with a front opening as probably the best Tantric outfit for a man, I can't resist quoting their other option: 'There are very few women who are not stirred by the primitive look and if you have a good physique, broad wristbands on both forearms, a bracelet around one of your biceps, a single ear-ring, broad belt and a loincloth should convey the right message.'

Even if the idea of you or your partner dressing in any of the above seems ludicrous or hysterically funny, don't dismiss it out of hand. If you want to deepen the quality of your relationship and experience greater levels of sexual fulfilment, you need to change patterns and attitudes.

In other words, if you want your sex life to stay exactly as it is, keep on doing what you are doing. If, on the other hand, you would like it to move forward to a higher plane of enjoyment and satisfaction, be prepared to try something different, even if you do have initial reservations.

RACHEL, 34, LECTURER

'One of the reasons that Tantra is perfect for me is that I can indulge my love of jewellery and nice clothes. I've always liked velvet and soft, touchable fabrics and dressing up like a goddess is heaven!'

MUSIC

Music is often an accompaniment to sex; Shakespeare spoke of its qualities as 'the food of love' and lovers old and new have been stirred by its power. Almost every couple has a special song or piece of music that they consider 'theirs' and music should never be under-rated for its capacity to enhance mood. Music appears capable of altering brain waves, which changes emotion and mood at a physiological level.

The slower your brain waves, the more calm and relaxed you feel. In such a state, you are more capable of living in the moment and thinking more clearly. Your skin is also more sensitive and responsive to touch and temperature. It is believed that music played at a rate of about 60 beats a minutes has the ability to lower heart rate, breathing and brain waves to the same level as during meditation. (This is slightly slower than the average resting heart rate of 72 to 80 beats a minutes.) Pieces by Mozart, Tchaikovsky and Chopin, as well as light jazz and most New Age music generally play at 60 beats a minute or slower. Rock is much faster, causing your brain waves to cycle faster and generally making you want to speed up whatever you happen to be doing. New Age music, which has a distinct rhythm, but little noticeable beat, tends to suspend your perception of time and space, and is therefore more likely to make you feel you could make love forever. No prizes for guessing which is the best accompaniment for Tantric lovemaking.

Most importantly, the music you play if you adopt a Tantric approach to sex

It's no use playing

Def Leppard, even if it's

your favourite track,

while trying to give

your partner a slow, sensual

massage. You'll end up battered and

defeated. But it might be the perfect

aural backdrop for a bit of wild

dancing round the living

room beforehand

should reflect your personal taste and moods of the moment. It's no use playing Def Leppard, even if it's your favourite track, while trying to give your partner a slow, sensual massage. You'll end up battered and defeated. But it might be the perfect aural backdrop for a bit of wild dancing round the living room beforehand.

The same rules apply to music as to all other aspects of Tantra: experiment with something new and see what you discover. Some people like listening to Indian classical music; others prefer the Western variety. If that's the case, the second act of Wagner's Tristan and Isolde; Berlioz's Symphonie Fantastique and the garden scene from Gounod's Faust, as well as old favourites such as Ravel's Bolero, have all been recommended by Tantric practitioners. One friend's personal favourites include Debussy's Après-midi d'un Faune and La Mer; Scheherezade (Rimsky-Korsakoff); Rite of Spring (Stravinsky); Romeo and Juliet (Prokofiev) and The Four Seasons (Vivaldi). Pop music can be equally effective. The Pointer Sisters singing 'I want a man with a slow hand'; Eric Clapton's 'You look wonderful tonight' and George Harrison's 'Something' are all guaranteed to work magic on some couples. If a song plucks at your heartstrings, include it in your Tantric lovemaking.

There is a lot of New Age music around now. Some of it is rather dull and repetitive, but some of it isn't and may feel absolutely right for you. Electronic classics such as Jean Michel Jarre's 'Oxygène' and 'Rainbow On Curved Air' by Terry Riley also have a lot to offer. Have fun experimenting with different sounds.

UNWINDING

'Getting into the mood' is not just about creating the right physical atmosphere for making love. You may have a perfect, warm and inviting room; candles may be lit and your favourite music may be playing on the CD. The love altar can be beautifully arranged and the scent of fresh flowers may fill the air. But if you are both stressed out and slightly annoyed with each other, having sex to release the pent-up tensions of the day is unlikely to bring you the mental bonding and lasting physical release you are seeking.

We frequently use sex as a way of unwinding. For some people, an orgasm is an effective sleeping pill, and there's nothing wrong with that. But when you are looking for greater intimacy in your relationship, making love to shake off stress and induce sleep won't get you there. It is too easy for your partner to feel 'dumped on'. The best time to make love is when you are feeling calm, relaxed and full of energy. Of course, this is an ideal. But it is a useful pointer to be aware of if you want more loving intimacy in your relationship. If you use anger or rows to stir up excitement in your lovemaking you may simply be fuelling these negative emotions and paving the way for more outbursts later on.

Bearing in mind that if you each approach making love with your partner with the idea of bringing them as much pleasure and possible, this in itself will reduce the chances of either of you feeling as though you are the accomplice to a slightly glorified bout of masturbation. This feeling of wanting to 'give first' is not about boring self-sacrifice that leads to resentment and grudges. It is about an openness of heart and mind and a willingness to see the best of your self reflected in your partner.

There is a lot to be said for treating your partner kindly in this way. The Dalai Lama has said, 'My religion is kindness.' We have all experienced the healing power of a kind act. What is so magical about kindness is that it transforms not only the lives of the people to whom it is directed, but also the life of the person who is being kind. I think the following story is a good illustration of this …

I recently met a woman called Celia who had looked after my godfather when he became ill. She lived next door, and every Saturday morning, she would invite him and his professional carer into her home for a glass of sherry and a chat, even when he was so frail and weak that he was scarcely able to make conversation. A few days after he died, I visited her with my father to thank her for what she had done.

I walked into her bungalow and I was instantly transported to somewhere special. It was like finding a small patch of heaven on earth. I stared at the colour of the walls and the weave of her curtains; what had she done with her interior design to achieve this magical effect? Never before had I felt so welcome or so instantly at ease in someone else's home.

Then I discovered her secret. Although she did not attend services at the village

If you are both stressed out and
slightly annoyed with each other,
having sex to release the pent-up
tensions of the day is unlikely to
bring you the mental bonding
and lasting physical release
you are seeking

church opposite, she cared for the fabric of the building and for the congregation as though they were her own family. Where other houses in the area boasted burglar alarms and heavy gates, Celia had a key in her front door with instructions on how to open it. People joined her for tea and toast before church on Sundays, and for coffee after the main service. Everyone was welcome. The people in the village knew that if ever they wanted some quiet space, they could drop by. 'I love coming in and finding someone sitting here having a cup of tea,' she explained.

After her husband's death, this elderly lady decided that her decent-sized home should be an open house. So she welcomed everyone. Celia fizzed with energy and humour, She wasn't pious or sanctimonious, but operated on the principle of the Dalai Lama – her religion was kindness. And as a result, she and her home resonated with love and peace.

If you can begin to treat your partner with this sort of loving kindness before you make love to them, you may not only change the quality of your sexual relationship, you can even change the quality of your surroundings, snowballing good thoughts and good feelings together.

While we tend to make a fuss of our partners in the early days together, familiarity breeds, if not contempt, a certain degree of laziness. This can take the edge off the sense that we are truly cared for and as a result, the level of intimacy between us slowly diminishes. The Tantra teacher Margo Anand has devised a game she calls 'the Yin and Yang Game', which is essentially an elaborate device to remind couples how to look after each other.

She specifies that for a certain period of time, one partner should meet all the requests of the other. Neither partner should request anything that will be detrimental to the other, and the partner who is doing the giving always reserves the right to gently refuse and ask for another task that they can fulfil with a happy heart. Anand recommends playing the game for a minimum of 6 hours, and, ideally, for 24 or 48. If this feels like too big a chunk of time for you to fit into your schedule, you can try with a shorter amount of time, remembering that it is the principle of playing it that will change your attitudes to each other.

R A C H E L , 3 4 , L E C T U R E R

'In relationships there are often a lot of compromises and grey areas where neither of you are getting what you really want; playing the game gives you the chance to give to your partner something they really would like, knowing that it will be your chance next to have something for yourself.

On one occasion I asked my boyfriend for a very gentle massage, more of an erotic touch than anything else, and then he wanted us to stand in front of each other, look into each other's eyes and listen to this very emotional song and to think of the other person's name when we heard it. Funnily enough, I thought he might ask for some weird sexual thing, but he didn't. Although what he asked for was very simple, it was quite scary because it felt so intimate. But we did it and that particular experience will always stick in my mind.'

The Heart Salutation or Namaste

Most of us in the West are familiar with some rituals, like shaking hands when we meet someone in a formal situation; we may even give 'mwah, mwah' air kisses on both cheeks, but few of us are familiar with the modern Tantric ritual inspired by the traditional Namaste (pronounced nah-mah-stay) greeting used in the East. While modern Easterners equate Namaste with saying 'Hi', Tantrics use it to signify a more spiritual greeting. In Tantra it means 'I honour the god within you' and it is a useful bridge between everyday life and a more spiritual approach to sex.

You may feel self-conscious at first, but sharing a Namaste with your partner is an excellent introduction to time spent together building a deeper level of intimacy and sexual fulfilment. If you don't have a partner, practise it in front of a mirror. This is how you do it:

Sit or stand opposite your partner with your hands loosely by your sides. Look into each other's eyes.

As you inhale, bring your hands together into a prayer position, with your thumbs roughly level with your breast bone (or heart centre). (As the Hindu sage, Ramana Maharshi noted, when a person wants to identify himself, he points to his chest.)

Maintaining eye contact for as long as you can, exhale gently forward from the waist until your foreheads touch. Hold this contact for a few moments.

Inhale slowly and straighten your back, keeping your hands cupped together against your chest. Looking deeply into your partner's eyes, say 'Namaste' and then let your hands drift back gently to your sides.

Ideally, the man should match the woman's breathing and follow the pace set by her. The most important thing is not to rush through it, but to take your time. (Incidentally, a loving and deliberate Namaste is a good summary of the Tantric approach to sex.)

The Kama Sutra

It's not essential to have a copy of the Kama Sutra on a bookshelf in your Tantric space, but it is an interesting read. It is the most famous book associated with Tantra, and like Tantra itself, it's the focus of a lot of misunderstanding. It was written in the fourth century by the Brahmin religious scholar, Mallinaga Vatsyayna, who collected the work of perhaps a dozen writers responsible for Tantric texts that had been passed down through the generations. Vatsyana added his own reflections on the laws and practices that governed life in India at the time.

The Kama Sutra is best known, of course, for its views on sex and the rules of love. But Vatsyayna was not solely concerned with sex and sexual positions. He created a guide for behaviour that stressed the physical, emotional and spiritual connection between men and women. He also included some less politically correct advice on how to dispose of your lover's marriage partner; the etiquette for being introduced to prostitutes and some deadly love potions.

Vatsyayna's work was first published in Britain in 1883 by the explorer Sir Richard Burton. Despite the fact that he ignored some of the commentaries and refused to translate them for fear of upsetting his Victorian readers, the former soldier and linguist, who spoke more than 40 languages, ensured that the Kama Sutra had an enduring impact on British society.

Following the success of his translation of the Kama Sutra (which he published anonymously through his Kama Shastra Society), Burton went on to translate the

Ananga Ranga, a 15th-century Hindu manuscript about the art of love, not dissimilar to the Kama Sutra, and the 16th-century Arabian book, *The Perfumed Garden*.

Although *The Perfumed Garden* was once considered on a par with the Kama Sutra, some of the anatomical details outlined in it are incorrect, and the assertion by the author, Sheikh Nefzawi, that a penis under 15 cm (6 in) long cannot offer a woman much satisfaction would probably be disputed by most men. *The Perfumed Garden* is unusual as an early sex manual in that it is a series of erotic stories filled with sexual fantasies. What it shares with the Kama Sutra, though, is the belief that women have as much right as men to sexual satisfaction, as the quotation below reveals:

'O you men, one and all, who are soliciting the love of woman and her affection, and who wish that sentiment in her heart to be of an enduring nature, play with her previous to intercourse; prepare her for enjoyment, and neglect nothing to attain that end. Explore her with the greatest care, and entirely occupied with her, let nothing else engage your thoughts. Do not let the moment best for pleasure pass away; that moment will be when you see her eyes moist, half closed. Then go to work, but remember, not until your kisses and playing have taken effect.'

It's advice that would not be out of place in a man's magazine today.

...explore her with the greatest care, and entirely occupied with her, let nothing else engage your thoughts...

7

MASSAGE, MEDITATION AND MUCH MORE ...

Touch is possibly one of the most under-rated human senses. Babies deprived of touch fail to thrive and I think the same applies to adults too. Massage enlivens our bodies, it stirs our emotions and it can make us feel connected and awake. While most people acknowledge that touch is important, we don't touch each other nearly enough. Studies have shown that without regular affectionate touch, women tend to become depressed and uninterested in sexual touch; while men become more aggressive and uninterested in touch that is not sexual.

If you are unable to make love through illness or some other reason, don't give up on touch as well. In the same way that the more sex we have, the more we welcome it, the more touch we receive, the more we benefit from it. Which is why it is dangerous to slip into a negative loop of not touching. When couples argue and stop having sex, they often stop touching each other too. This creates an emotional distance between them, which makes it harder to resolve the problems they are facing.

When we touch each other, a hormone called oxytocin is released into the bloodstream, decreasing stress levels and increasing sex hormones. In women this raises sexual responsiveness and in men it boosts the sensitivity of their penis and improves their erection.

Massage, or caring and deliberate touch, can be a form of meditation. Not only does it instil deep levels of relaxation, but between lovers it can build a powerful emotional connection. By stilling your mind, and focusing only on the sensations in your body when receiving a massage, you can achieve a level of mental openness that enables you to reach higher levels of physical and mental fulfilment than you may have thought possible. Equally, when you are giving a massage, focusing on loving energy flowing out of your hands and into your partner's body, can turn touch into an ecstatic and healing experience.

If you've ever experienced a wonderful professional massage and slid off the couch afterwards, either in a state of warm relaxation or feeling exhilarated and ready for anything, imagine the intense power of a massage that not only felt great but came with a soundtrack of love and compliments from your partner. Most couples are pretty half-hearted when it comes to giving each other a massage.

Either they don't know how to do it properly or they offer a quick rub of the shoulder blades before switching to what seems like the more exciting business of having sex.

This is a fast food approach to lovemaking, where you skip the formalities of the linen tablecloth, wine glasses and lovingly prepared food, in favour of getting your hunger sated immediately. Of course, there's nothing wrong with fast food. It fills you up with instant fuel for your body to work with. But if you only eat burgers and chips, you are depriving yourself of a whole world of exquisite tastes, smells and textures. Exactly the same principle applies to sex. For a few people, making love in the same bed, in the same way, with the same person at the same time of the week is a good enough sex life. For most of us, repetition leads to staleness and boredom. As a result, people either give up on sex altogether or seek the excitement that they once shared with their partner with someone new. Novelty value has a surprisingly big pull. The fact that so many Western marriages end in divorce is testament to this. But people who practise Tantra have other more fulfilling and life-enhancing choices.

Tantra encourages you to take the time to find new ways of pleasing your partner, inside and outside bed. Instead of both shutting down on each other as the stresses and strains of modern life take over, and possibly even ending your journey together in the divorce courts under a cloud of bitterness and resentment, you can choose to reawaken the sense of attraction that first brought you together.

In Tantra, the fact that you know someone well is a bonus in your sexual relationship; not a disadvantage. For some people, giving someone a loving massage feels even more intimate than having sex with them. This is principally because a massage between lovers requires you to give from your heart, and a huge number of people make love only with their genitals – their hearts are cut off from the whole experience.

If you intend to share a massage with your partner, there are a few ground rules that need to be followed. The first is that the room should be warm and welcoming – you can't expect someone to relax if they are in a cold, inhospitable environment. Light candles, waft a stick of incense around (or buy scented candles and save yourself the effort) and, ideally, pull a mattress onto the floor. Giving a massage on the floor is preferable to a bed because it is much easier for the giver to move around. If you can't face the thought of shifting the bedroom mattress onto the floor (mine feels as heavy as a small car) then invest in some big, soft cushions that are comfortable to lie on. Cover these with a sheet or some fabric that it's fine to spill massage oil on. Finally, make sure that you have removed any jewellery that might snag on your partner's skin, and that your fingernails are smooth, and you are in business.

One important point to remember if you are giving a massage is that you should always remain comfortable and calm. It is tempting to hunch your shoulders or twist your spine awkwardly if a particular stroke seems to be giving a great deal of pleasure and the recipient wants you to carry on. But the moment you start to feel uncomfortable you should shift your position so that you are able to breathe deeply and easily. This will influence the quality of the massage more than you might think.

If you have never given or received a massage before, it can be a good idea to start by giving your partner and hand and foot massage. This is usually intensely pleasurable for the recipient, and doesn't feel as daunting for the giver as being confronted by an entire naked body when you are not quite sure where to start.

HAND AND FOOT MASSAGE

As ever, both the masseur and the person receiving the massage should shower or bath before beginning. You should allow about 20 minutes to massage both hands or feet and give your partner plenty of time to relax afterwards. The whole process should last around half an hour.

Aromatherapy oils are good for hand and foot massage; almond and grapeseed are excellent standbys, especially if you add a few drops of lavender oil. You can buy high quality massage oils that prevent linen stains and are easily washed away. Alternatively, vitamin E cream or aloe vera lotion can also work well.

Begin the massage with the intention that you want to bring a relaxing, healing experience to your partner. Even if you are planning to make love later, put this out of your mind; otherwise you will be tempted to treat the massage as an obstacle to

Reflexologists consider that their form of therapeutic foot massage is an effective method of healing the whole body as particular areas of the feet relate to specific parts of the body. The big toe, for example, is understood to link to the pituitary and pineal glands. Tantrics believe that pituitary stimulation harmonizes the physical dimension of our sexual response and that stimulating the pineal gland harmonizes the emotions connected with our sexuality be got out of the way before the fun begins. Whereas in reality, by taking time to nourish your partner in this way, you will be hugely increasing your chances of having a great deal more fun when you become sexual with each other.

If you are massaging the hands, massage both hands entirely, including the wrists. Work your way slowly across one hand and finish it before you start on the other. Press as deeply and firmly as you can, without causing pain. Knead each tiny area, as if the skin was covered with a fine grid of small squares and you wanted to make sure you covered every single square on the hand. Maintain a continuous flow. Think of sculpting your lover's body, rather than imposing on it.

One way to start a foot massage is to press your knuckles firmly into the sole, covering it with small, circling movements, then work over the foot again, this time using your thumbs. Now gently bend the toes forward and back, before massaging the top of the foot with your thumbs. Supporting the foot with one hand, run the tip of your thumb down the grooves of the foot. Don't massage the ankle itself as you should avoid massaging directly on top of a bone.

Big toe massage sounds bizarre, but there are plenty of people who will testify to the pleasure that it can bring. Some people find having their big toe sucked extremely arousing and this can lead to pleasant sensations spreading out in waves across the whole body.

Reflexologists consider that their form of therapeutic foot massage is an effective method of healing the whole body as particular areas of the feet relate to specific parts of the body. The big toe, for example, is understood to link to the pituitary and pineal glands. Tantrics believe that pituitary stimulation harmonizes the physical dimension of our sexual response and that stimulating the pineal gland harmonizes the emotions connected with our sexuality.

Whole body massage

Always remember to warm your hands and your massage oil before giving any type of massage, but this especially applies when you intend to massage the whole of your partner's body. You can gently warm the massage oil by standing the bottle in a bowl of warm water and washing your hands in warm water before you begin. If you are uncertain how to touch your partner, ask them what they would like. Often people touch you the way they would like to be touched, so recall previous sensual experiences with them and try this theory out.

The basic sequence of a full body massage is to begin working on the back and focus on the smaller areas such as the shoulder blades, upper back, lower back and buttocks, then along either side of the spine (but don't ever apply pressure directly on to the spine). Next massage each leg, first upwards, then downwards, before shifting your attention to each foot.

Then your partner rolls over onto their back, leaving you to bring pleasure to their shoulders and neck, each arm – including the wrist, hand and fingers – and finally the abdomen and the fronts of the legs. As an optional extra, some people like their scalp, face and ears massaged, but it's usually wise to check beforehand exactly what your partner's requirements are. (According to Chinese medicine, the ears are filled with acupuncture points and are very sensitive to touch, tongues and even warm breath.) Also, bear in mind that some people don't like massage oil in their hair (especially if it's newly washed and they don't fancy looking like they've been plugged into the nearest socket).

A FOOLPROOF MASSAGE THAT (NEARLY) EVERY WOMAN WILL LOVE ...

One version of a full body massage that most women love is to begin massaging down both sides of her spine to her lower back. This brings warm energy to her pelvis. Next, work around the centre of her chest, firstly with your thumbs and then with the palms of your hands, using firm but gentle circular motions; this induces calm and helps open the heart. Move from here down to her belly and then on to her pubic bone, the area covered by the base chakra, which is associated with sexuality and creativity; and finally massage her inner legs, moving from the ankle upwards. This arouses the energy line that begins at the big toe and moves up the centre of her leg to her groin area. And, while we are talking about women, a word here for the nape of the neck. This is an erogenous zone for lots of women that is often ignored. Delicate kisses and gentle rubbing and licking here can have a big impact on your partner's delight-meter.

Try and tune in to your partner's body and what they would enjoy. Some people like to chat during a massage, but this isn't ideal as it prevents the recipient from concentrating on and relaxing into their physical sensations.

There are several different kinds of massage strokes:

- **Fan strokes**: Rest both palms flat on each side of the spine. Steadily slide your hands upwards for a distance of 15cm (6 inches) and move them softly towards the sides of the body, so that they mould to the rib-cage before pulling them back downwards. Bring your hands back to the start of the stroke and then glide them up the back and repeat the same pattern.
- **Circle strokes**: Place both hands parallel but slightly apart, fingers pointing away from you on the back or the belly. Slide steadily in a clockwise circular motion, with the right hand leading, then lift your right hand to allow the left one to make a continuous circular motion. Pass your right hand over the left wrist before dropping it back down to complete a half-circle motion. Continue the circle strokes so that they spiral over the skin in a smooth, unbroken wave.
- **Percussion**: This is a stimulating form of massage that tones the skin and improves circulation. Using the edges of your hands, make a rapid succession of strokes so that your hands bounce lightly up and down on your partner's body.
- **Feathering**: Brush your fingertips lightly over your partner's skin. There are experts who say that the lighter the touch, the more powerful the effect. With this stroke you are working on an energetic rather than a deep muscular level. Feathering is a fun and pleasing way to bring your massage towards an end.

As a general principle, repeat each sequence of strokes three times before gliding into the next movement. You can use a towel or sheet to cover the parts of your partner's body you are not touching, so that they stay warm. (A warm towel over the lower back – the kidney area – may boost sexual desire as well as relaxation.) When you have completed your final strokes, place both hands flat on your partner's body and stand quietly, allowing everything to settle gently.

LINDA, 34, MARKETING MANAGER

'The best massage I ever had was with my partner when we just held our hands millimetres above each other's bodies. You can actually start to feel the electricity between you. If you do it and you are both naked, it is very sexy, and you can get turned on without even touching each other. I thought that was amazing.'

TANTRIC MASSAGE

The main difference between conventional massage and Tantric massage is that Tantrics use more than their hands to give pleasure. Feathers; hair (either head or chest); soft silky fabrics and butterfly kisses can all be trailed across your partner's body to bring them deepening levels of delight. (On a practical note, introduce feathers or silky fabrics before you apply massage oil. Not only will they feel more pleasant on the receiver's skin, you won't have to worry about how you are going to remove oil stains afterwards.)

Equally, talking to your partner, and whispering the things that you love and appreciate about them as you caress them can also have a liberating and pleasurable effect. I can't stress enough that you should only say positive and loving things – now is not the time to ask them if they've remembered to put out the dustbin or cancel the papers.

SARAH, 41, OPTICIAN

'Sometimes I don't think that I really want to make love, and then my partner begins to massage me and it just smooths my anxieties away. I find that I get back in touch with my body and that means I am more likely to get turned on. Also, I don't start to make love feeling under pressure because I'm doing it for him and not especially for me. At the end of a sensual massage, I want to pounce!'

THE ART OF EROTIC KISSING

Richard Craze, the author of *Tantric Sexuality: A Beginner's Guide*, believes that one of the ways we can best experience energy consciously is when we are kissing. Let's be honest, most Western teenagers stick their tongue down someone's throat and

SIMPLY BREATHE MORE DEEPLY

FROM YOUR BELLY, RATHER THAN

THE TOP HALF

OF YOUR

CHEST, AND

RELAX, RATHER

THAN TENSE, YOUR MUSCLES, AS

YOU DO SO. IF THIS IS THE ONLY

THING YOU

TAKE AWAY

FROM TANTRA,

IT WILL PAY

DIVIDENDS, BOTH IN YOUR SEX

LIFE AND IN THE EVERYDAY WORLD

hope for the best. But erotic kissing is a skill that takes time to learn and lots of practice. In China, couples won't kiss in front of other people as they regard it as something so intimate and sexual that for them it would be like making love in public. Richard Craze suggests that you agree with your partner to spend as much time practising erotic kissing as you can. He suggests:

'You can use your lips and tongue to explore your partner's mouth. You can suck the tongue, lick the inside of the lips, nip with your teeth, even exchange saliva – known as the 'juice of jade' in China. You can use your tongue to explore your lover's entire face: lick the eyelids, the ears and underside of the chin (this is particularly erotic). If you and your partner suck each other's tongue in turn you may find it quite easy to orgasm spontaneously.

Another aspect of erotic kissing is to use your fingers too. As you lick and suck on your partner's mouth you can both insert your fingers into each other's mouth and suck on the fingers as well. Obviously, in all of these exercises some degree of personal hygiene is important. Clean your teeth beforehand, wash your hands and avoid strong tasting or smelling foods.

You can use your tongue to explore your partner's hands. The skin between the fingers is especially sensitive. Most men report that having their thumbs sucked is very erotic both because of its resemblance to oral sex but also because of the sensitivity of the thumb.'

This is a far cry from the clumsy, teeth-crashing snog, which is the introduction to kissing for most Westerners.

BREATHING

Breath is the crucial link between the mind, the body and the spirit. On one level it's easy to dismiss the notion of breathing as anything more than a necessary physiological function – if you don't breathe, you die and that's it. But this is only part of the picture. In many cultures, from Aboriginal to Hebrew, breath is synonymous with the spirit and even in English the word 'inspiration' literally means 'to breathe in'.

Until a couple of centuries ago, a dying person's last breath was considered to be their soul leaving the body. The ancient Romans encouraged all close relatives to lean over a dying person to breath in their essence. In modern times, breathing is used as pain relief for women in labour and just about anyone will recommend that you 'take a deep breath' before you plunge into any important situation, whether it's giving a presentation or starting an exam. What we have become less familiar with, though, is the experience of energy rushing through the body as a result of conscious breathing, leading to an altered state of mind that hovers between the joyous and the ecstatic.

There are many techniques that you can learn to enhance your lovemaking by altering the way that you breathe, but one you can try almost immediately is to simply breathe more deeply from your belly, rather than the top half of your chest, and to relax, rather than tense, your muscles, as you do so. In fact, if this is the only thing you take away from Tantra, it will pay dividends, both in your sex life and in the everyday world. Most of us breathe shallowly and irregularly, using less than a third of our lung capacity. This means we take in only a small amount of oxygen. As a result we have lower energy levels and toxins build up more easily in the body. In effect, you don't have enough octane in your fuel mix. Psychotherapists often observe that people in psychological pain restrict their breathing in order to anaesthetize themselves. This can become a pattern that they learn to live with, but it prevents them fully experiencing pleasure and joy in their sexual relationships.

We inhale more than 20,000 breaths over a 24-hour period. (According to yogic texts it is 21,600). If we breathe correctly, we can help maintain our energy levels, keep a clear mind and build a healthy body. The most basic breathing technique is called The Complete Breath, or the Healing Breath.

The Complete Breath

The simplest way to experience this is to lie on your back on the floor, with your body warm, comfortable and relaxed. Place the palm of your left hand over your heart and the palm of your right hand over your navel. Close your mouth and your eyes.

Begin by exhaling any stale air left in your body out through your nose. Then, as you breathe in, imagine sending the air from your nose deep into your belly, and allow your belly to swell and expand. (As your tummy moves outwards, your diaphragm moves down and massages your abdominal organs.) Retain the breath for a count of 4. When you breathe out, concentrate on contracting your belly first and then emptying your lungs from the bottom upwards. As your belly contracts, your diaphragm moves up and massages your heart.

You breathe in and out through your nose during this exercise, so that the air is warmed and filtered before it enters your lungs. Breathing through your mouth introduces cold air to the body, which is harder for your body to work with.

One of the trickier things for Westerners to do is to relax their tummy muscles so that their belly moves in and out freely. Apart from the fact that a lot of us carry a lot of tension in this area of our bodies, as a culture we tend to be obsessed with flat stomachs, and as a result many women, especially, try and hold their stomachs in most of the time. If you find breathing this way difficult to begin with, rent a video or see a comedian who makes you rock with laughter. This will ensure that your abdomen will relax and play its proper role in breathing quite naturally.

A few minutes of this kind of conscious belly breathing each day will teach your body to breathe deeply, even when you are asleep. As far as men are concerned, deep breathing helps control if or when they ejaculate. The simple reason for this is that breathing is directly connected to heart rate. If you are breathing quickly and shallowly – say, if you have been running – your heart rate increases. If you are breathing deeply and slowly, your heart rate decreases. Generally speaking, we breathe twice as fast during sex. So if you are a man who wants to control your arousal rate – and therefore your ejaculation – one of the keys to this is deep and slow breathing.

Note: If you become dizzy while you are practising this or any other kind of breathing technique, stop and let your breathing pattern return to normal.

The heart breath

Practising a breathing exercise with someone else can be fun and a rewarding prelude to making love. The Heart Breath is a particularly powerful exercise to do with your partner, but it's a good idea to practise it on your own first, to get the hang of it, before you try it with someone else. You can do this standing, sitting with a straight back or lying down with your knees bent. You may like to put on some soft, tender music while you do this exercise. There are a few simple steps to follow:

- Close your eyes and place your hands on your heart. This helps you focus on sending energy to this area.
- As you breathe in, imagine drawing energy into your heart.
- Pause at the end of the in-breath, and focus on your heart.
- Release your breath, and slowly breathe out.
- Continue breathing like this for several minutes.

You may feel a tingling in your heart area, or you may feel nothing at all. It doesn't matter. Don't let your brain turn over hundreds of thoughts about whether it's 'working' or not. Every time you feel your concentration start to slip, just gently bring yourself back into the present and think about your heart. Some people find it helpful to visualize the colour pink as they breathe in and out.

Once you feel comfortable with this exercise, and you are increasingly aware of your heart area, you'll be ready to practise it with a partner. Begin with a Heart Salutation or 'Namaste' (see page 182) and keep eye contact with your partner throughout. This isn't as easy as it sounds. If you feel awkward or self-conscious, just close your eyes and concentrate on following your own breathing pattern, as you did when you were alone. To begin with, this exercise is easier if you stand:

Gaze into each other's eyes

- Place your right hand on your partner's heart.
- With your out-breath, imagine breathing the energy from your heart into their heart. (Picturing this as pink or gold light may help.)
- With your in-breath, imagine inhaling their heart energy into your heart.
- Once you feel comfortable with this, try breathing alternately. In other words, as you breathe out, they breathe in. This way, loving energy is circulated between you.

Don't worry if you struggle to find the right rhythm at first. Most of us are unused to this kind of exercise and initially it's easy to feel embarrassed or uncertain. But, as with most things in life, it is your intention that really matters. If you embark on this exercise with the intention of becoming closer to your partner, no matter how many times you get the giggles or you feel that you aren't making the grade, it won't detract from the spirit of the exercise, which is to bring you closer together.

PRIYATAMA, 52, SEX THERAPIST

'*Sometimes my partner and I just cuddle up to one another in bed and breathe together and there's a lovely feeling of our bodies connecting, as though we share one breath. It is like a circle of deep connection. Occasionally, that's all we do and then we just drift off to sleep, enjoying that kind of gentle contact, and although it might sound a bit corny, that in itself is very special.*'

Meditation

Someone once defined prayer as talking and meditation as listening. I don't know whether they added 'to yourself and God' at the end of that sentence, but if you do I think the description makes even more sense. Meditation focuses the mind in a state of relaxed awareness. But even though meditation is linked with spirituality, you don't have to believe in God in order to receive its physical and psychological benefits.

There are many different kinds of meditation. Simply sitting still with your back straight, closing your eyes and following the progress of your breath is one approach; others are slightly more complicated but can be mastered relatively easily. Some meditators say that it is helpful if you receive a mantra meditation from a strong, established tradition so that you can be supported in the early stages of learning to meditate.

Although it is fairly common for people to mix up deep relaxation with meditation, they are not one and the same thing. Deep relaxation induces a state of calmness, which is necessary to meditation, but meditation actually brings a clarity of mind that is not always present when you are simply in a state of moderate or even deep relaxation. So although it is important to take time to relax and do things that you find fun, which in turn make you less tense or stressed, this is not the same as meditating.

If you have never meditated before, you can begin by setting some time aside (10 to 15 minutes should be enough to start) when you can be by yourself and away from the distractions of the TV, telephone and other people. It will help to find a chair that supports your back so that you can sit with a straight spine and put your feet flat onto the floor. Sit with your palms loosely in your lap; some people prefer to turn them facing upwards.

You may find it helpful if you decide how long you want to meditate for before you begin. With time, you will find you can tune into your internal body clock and you will be surprised at how accurate it is. Experienced meditators report that they simply set a time to finish inside their heads and find that they open their eyes at the time they have chosen. If you are just beginning to meditate, though, you may not want to rely on this method, so a muffled alarm clock can be handy. One friend set the alarm on his mobile phone and found that worked for him.

Mantra meditation

The universe is made up of vibrations; mantras are syllables or phrases, composed of consonants and vowels that are considered to have particularly potent sound. Mantra meditation – in which mantras are regularly repeated – has been scientifically proven to raise pain thresholds and reduce biological age. The theory is that during meditation the pattern of your brainwaves alters and is replaced by other calming, chemical responses. In some European countries, regular meditators are awarded lower premiums by life assurance companies.

The best-known mantra is probably 'Om'. This sound is made up of three parts – AH...OO...MM. Whether you say it out loud or inside your head, the AH should come from deep inside you; the OO is short and the MM should be the longest sound. If you say it aloud you will feel it resonate through your head. Although I'd recommend a spiritual mantra that has some meaning for you, one American research group taught students to meditate reasonably well using the words 'Coca-cola', so if you shy away from anything that sounds too spiritual, it doesn't mean that meditation is not for you. Try different words, sounds or phrases and see what works best.

Interestingly, scientists have discovered that some people begin to acquire the qualities of the word they use to meditate on. (I can't imagine how that would apply to 'Coca cola' – fizzy and refreshing, perhaps?) Mantras such as 'peace', 'joy' and 'patience' have been used and the results monitored in terms of brainwaves, circulation, pulse and other physical effects. Checks on the psychological state of mantra meditators have found that people who practise regularly also become more peaceful and less liable to angry reactions. Their overall state of their health is improved too, particularly in relation to diseases associated with stress.

Buddhist meditation

The following Buddhist meditation is a good one to try to begin with. Start thinking of yourself as someone that you love. Wish yourself well in every way and flood your body with thoughts of love and compassion. As you breathe in, fill your mind with thoughts of peace; as your breathe out, let go of stress and tension. Inside your head, say the words 'May I be well and happy and may my mind be at peace.'

Then think of someone you love. Send them your love and compassion and wish them well. Inside your head say 'May they be well and happy, and may their minds be at peace. Advocates of this particular meditation suggest that you then think of someone you don't know well; someone you don't like or resent, and people to the north, south, east and west of you and that you repeat the same sentiment for everyone.

You close by saying or thinking 'May all beings be well and happy. May they know joy and peace, love and compassion. May any merit gained from this practice be shared with them, and may they attain their Supreme goal'. And finally, you remember with gratitude 'I am one of those beings'.

If this seems rather complicated, just repeat a one-word mantra for 10 to 20 minutes. When other thoughts come into your mind, as they invariably will, simply acknowledge them and let them go. Meditation is not about 'doing'. Don't try and judge your efforts, either. Sometimes it is easy to slip into a deeply relaxed and tranquil state; at other times it feels like water trickling through your fingers. As Westerners we tend to want immediate results, or at least a 'quick-fix'. Meditation repays you over time. And the less you 'try' the simpler it becomes.

As you become more accustomed to the stillness you acquire through meditation, the easier you will find it to focus your attention on your body and your heart during Tantric sex and to expand into greater levels of pleasure. As the psychoanalyst Fritz Perls said, you can 'Lose your mind and come to your senses'.

Dynamic meditation

Meditation does not necessarily involve sitting still. Moving meditations have been practised over the centuries by people who find them effective, not just for stilling the mind, but for keeping the body fit too. Osho, the maverick guru and philosopher who triggered a revival of interest in Tantra in the West, taught one particular type of dynamic meditation that may not appeal to the faint-hearted, but is a brilliant wake-up call for the body and mind.

The first time I was introduced to this, I was sceptical about its benefits. Basically, it lasts for an hour and is divided into four distinct phases. The first 10 minutes is spent breathing 'chaotically' to a background of rapid drumming music, which becomes increasingly wild over the next 10 minutes. This means you breathe

...imagine that you are growing roots down into the ground, either from the base of your spine, if you are sitting cross-legged, or through the soles of your feet. Imagine these are energetic roots, reaching deep into the earth...

erratically and pump oxygen into your lungs by flapping your arms (if you are old enough to recall hideous memories of dancing 'The Funky Chicken' you are not far off).

For the next 10 minutes, people are encouraged to 'cathart'. This may mean screaming, punching a cushion or whatever takes your fancy – assuming that it involves you and no one else. (For most self-conscious Brits this is probably harder than running a marathon. More of my thoughts on this later.) The next 10 minutes are spent jumping up and down with your arms in the air shouting 'Ho', to a steady, throbbing beat, followed by another 10 minutes of silence and physical stillness, brought to a close by some gentle dancing and stretching to greet the day.

This is how dynamic meditation works: The combination of breathing and jumping to music sends the meditator into a blissful trance by whizzing energy through the body. (Joggers are often familiar with the similar experience of their minds clearing and experiencing a 'high' a couple of kilometres into a long run.) When the vigorous movement stops, the thoughts in the brain have been stilled, and the meditator simply drops into a state of deep peace and relaxation. The dancing then wakes you up to face the day.

My first impressions of this dynamic meditation confirmed every prejudice I had about cult-type behaviour and general weirdness. But after suppressing the urge to laugh when I pictured various friends' faces if they could see me jumping up and down shouting 'Ho', I decided to go with the flow and see what happened. During the silence, I found myself by an open door. Initially, I was slightly cross, thinking I'd picked a bad place to stand and that I would get cold. But within seconds, a wonderful feeling of warmth had worked its way up my spine to the top of my neck. It was as though I was standing underneath an electric heater (I wasn't). Then I had the impression of someone about a head and shoulders taller than me standing behind me; the presence was not in the slightest bit threatening. In fact, it felt hugely reassuring. The feeling was so good, that when the music started and people began to move, I felt faintly disappointed that it was going to end. But the warm sensation around my neck lasted for the next few hours, and the belief that dynamic meditation has much to offer has lasted ever since.

As we've already established, the principles of Tantra are not restricted to sexual relationships. The attitude of 'giving love first' is part of a wider picture. Meditation is part of Tantra and can play a useful role in the rest of your life too.

BERNADETTE, 31, TEACHER

'Practising Tantra and the Buddhist exercises of developing loving kindness has changed my life quite dramatically. You appreciate that you can't do this stuff in isolation from everything else. When you say 'May all beings be well; may all beings be happy; may all beings be free from the causes of suffering' you realize that sexual feelings should not be shunned or repressed. In fact, they should be channelled and celebrated so you can become integrated as a whole person. I feel like I have woken up. I have so much more energy and I laugh a lot more too.'

If you still feel that meditation may not be for you, take note of one Cambridge scientist's recommendation that the NHS should prescribe meditation for patients. He studied the results of patients at risk of heart attacks who meditated for at least an hour a week for four years and found that they had significantly reduced their blood pressure and showed fewer symptoms of heart disease after the control period. He compiled a list of danger signs and suggested that anyone who suffers from any of the following should consider signing up for meditation:

- always rushing about
- losing your sense of humour
- being unable to make decisions and stick to them
- growing impatient
- becoming increasingly forgetful
- feeling tense and irritable
- nagging
- constantly criticizing others
- hating sitting around doing nothing
- not really listening to other people because your mind is spinning with your own problems.

If you really don't think you have time for meditation, the next time you are on a plane and you are feeling stressed out, close your eyes and try imaging that you are filling the plane and becoming bigger and bigger until the plane is part of you. Then imagine that you are outside in the big sky, which is becoming smaller as you become bigger and eventually become absorbed into the entire universe. You may find this unexpectedly easy. For some reason, the higher the altitude, the easier it is to meditate. So perhaps that accounts for the monks and wise women who have made their way to mountain tops for centuries.

HEAVEN AND EARTH MEDITATION

One particularly powerful Tantric meditation is taught by Tantra teacher Leora. It is called the Heaven and Earth meditation and its effectiveness lies in the way that it connects your spirituality and your body, and so increases your ability to expand your sexual experience. Either read it aloud to your partner, put it on to tape or buy Leora's CD (details of which can be found at the back of this book).

First, get comfortable, either cross-legged on the floor, or sitting in a chair with your feet on the ground and your back straight. Now imagine that you are growing roots down into the ground, either from the base of your spine, if you are sitting cross-legged, or through the soles of your feet. Imagine these are energetic roots, reaching deep into the earth.

As you breathe in and out, visualize these roots expanding and stretching through the layers of earth and rock, until you can start to sense the heat coming from the centre of the earth. It might help to imagine the colour red as you do this. With each out-breath allow your roots to grow deeper and deeper – into the molten lava at the centre of the earth. Feel the intense heat and imagine that through this heat you're contacting the hot, fiery core of the earth, symbolizing your connection to this source of life.

Then, as you continue to breathe, draw up this heat and redness into your body. Think of it as your passion, or your lust for life, and your desire to be alive in your body, here and now. Keep breathing and drawing this energy up through your roots, right into the soles of your feet.

Allow the warmth to permeate up your legs. Draw that red-hot energy into your pelvis, allowing it to burn away anything that is not aligned with your love of life, with joy, and with vibrancy. Breathe in, drawing that heat into your abdomen. Imagine it burning away any obstacles to your being fully in tune with your passion, or your vitality.

Next, draw that energy into your lungs and chest, allowing your lungs to expand with the fullness of life, celebrating life. Breathe into the centre of your chest, in the area of your heart. Feel your heart expand with your breath, and get hot, full of passion for life and love. Allow the fire to burn in your heart, burning away any obstacles to love.

Pull the energy into the crown area at the top of your head. Now visualize growing branches that reach up into the sky. Feel these energetic channels stretching into the cool white fire of the universe – the realm beyond mortal life; the realm of the infinite.

Draw the cool white fire of the infinite down through the branches into the crown at the top of your head. Open up your crown area to allow the cool white fire of the universe to rain down on your head like sparks. Feel the sense of infinite possibilities for you, the sense of spaciousness, and of expansion.

Bring this sense of spaciousness into your chest. Let your heart be soothed and allow your heart to open up. Imagine the cool white fire of the heavens burning together with the hot red fire of earth in your heart, mixing and mingling in the heat. See your heart as a meeting point. You are a bridge between heaven and earth.

As you breathe out, allow the energy of this red and white heat to expand, allowing a sense of love to fill your heart. If you have a partner, let this feeling of love to flow out from your heart towards your partner, and from your partner to the whole world beyond. As you breathe in, imagine receiving love. Breathe in and out, receiving and giving love.

Awakening the senses

It's disturbing how much 21st century living dulls our senses. Many of us live in the equivalent of insulated boxes. Our offices and cars are air-conditioned; our homes are centrally heated and we lead such busy, work–orientated lives that few of us have time to appreciate the changing seasons or even to walk through the woods and kick a pile of leaves. Many of us live under the impression that Nature is something to shrink from or control, rather than something to embrace, and as a result our five physical senses are greatly diminished.

Tantra is about awakening our senses. We can aim to do this through making love with another person, and a sexual relationship with finely tuned senses is greatly enhanced. But we need help to get there. And this is where Tantric technique can play a part. In the Awakening the Senses exercise each partner introduces the other to a range of sensory experiences beyond their normal realm. If you've ever seen the film *Nine-and-a-Half Weeks*, you may recall a scene in which the leading actress was blindfolded and fed by her lover while both were in a highly erotic state. The story of the film – a brief, highly charged passionate affair – is actually a pretty shallow, one-dimensional picture of how a relationship can be, but the memory of that scene lingers in the minds of many people who watched the movie.

In the loving, Tantric version of this experience, it is not only the sense of taste that is stimulated, but all five senses. Ideally, you should allow at least an hour for this, leaving a minute or so between each stimulus. It doesn't have to be something you do before making love, in fact it can work well if you remove that expectation. Instead, just concentrate on fully experiencing the sensations of the moment and feel your senses expand to bring you increasing levels of pleasure.

Firstly, you need to create a food tray for your partner. Don't panic if you are not a Jamie Oliver standard chef; all you need is a selection of fruit (check with your partner beforehand what their dislikes are and make sure you avoid those). Then you need to prepare your room, light candles and incense, make sure it is warm and welcoming and that your partner has somewhere comfortable to sit on the floor. (Use plenty of cushions for support if you want them to sit on a bed.)

Blindfold your partner with a soft scarf and lead them into the room, explaining that he or she has no need to talk; all that is required of them is that they breathe deeply, relax and sink into the experiences on offer. Our initial experiences are often visual, and by removing this sense with a blindfold, we heighten our awareness of the other senses.

Hearing:

Put on some of your favourite music, or if you have musical instruments in the house play them softly. Ring bells and let their sound vibrate around the room. This is an occasion for pleasurable noises only, so avoid bangs and crashes and any sound that might cause your partner to be alarmed. (Make sure the answerphone is switched on and the mobiles are turned off – you don't want everyday noise intruding on your time together.)

Smell:

Pass perfumes and essential oils under your partner's nose, without touching their skin. Let them smell each one individually; make sure you wait a minute before you move on to the next scent as a clash of smells can be overwhelming. Peppermint is a good one to start with, you can move on to more exotic fragrances later, depending on your partner's personal taste. If you can change the music without too much fuss, put on a CD of natural sounds, such as running water or waves rushing on to the shore.

Taste:

Offer small mouthfuls of fruit to your partner, brushing their lips with it before gently popping it into their mouths. Kiwifruit, avocadoes, mangoes and strawberries are ideal. You can dip the fruit in a drink – anything from cordial, if that's what your partner likes, to champagne, if it's within your budget – and then rub their lips with the bite-sized piece of fruit before allowing it to enter their mouths very, very slowly. You can also drip a tiny amount of honey on to their lips, or caress their lips with a finger dipped in wine or something chocolatey (the inside of a chocolate truffle is perfect for this …)

Touch:

Collect a selection of feathers and fabrics, such as velvet, fur and silk. Gently stroke the fabric across your partner's arms, cheeks, neck, feet and ankles. Move slowly, as this will increase your partner's sensitivity to touch. You can also blow softly on parts of their body, use your hair to tickle their skin or lightly run your fingertips across their body. Be inventive and have fun; but remember, it is your partner's experience that matters most. So even if you think you have a brilliant idea to awaken their senses, if you have the slightest suspicion that they may not enjoy it, don't think of trying it out.

When you feel the time is right, change the music to something that touches both your hearts. Gather together the food, the fabrics and whatever else you have used in the exercise and add a couple of lit candles (being sure to keep the candles well away from anything flammable.) Sit behind your partner, rest your right hand over their heart and cradle them in your arms.

Sight:

To end the ritual, remove your partner's blindfold, try not to speak or ask 'How was it for you?' Just allow your partner to get used to seeing things again, then look into each other's eyes and enjoy a hug.

The suggestions above are simply ideas – you don't have to follow them. In fact, it is important that you take your partner's preferences into account and that you cater to their individual tastes. One of the by-products of this exercise is to build trust and intimacy between you. You can, if you like, swap roles over the same evening, but sometimes it can be good to do this exercise on different days, so that the person who is receiving can just enter into it wholeheartedly, without planning how they will return the favour later that same night. Equally, the same thinking can apply to the 'giver'. There is a lot of pleasure to be had from giving someone else a lovely time, and it doesn't hurt to enter fully into that experience for a whole evening too.

8

WHEN YOU'VE LOST THAT LOVING FEELING...

The list of problems people associate with sex is long and complex: wobbly erections; premature ejaculation; lack of desire and worries about ageing. Suffering from just one of the above can be enough to put you off sex altogether. Some people may feel even more traumatised by an earlier, abusive relationship. Nevertheless, Tantra can still offer a path of healing and reconnection.

Many sexual problems can be overcome with the help of sex therapists and relationship counsellors, but appointments can be hard to come by, and not everyone feels at home discussing intimate details of their lives with a stranger. Far too many people soldier on, either hoping their problems will go away or else give up on sex altogether.

Naturally, if celibacy is a conscious choice, and it feels entirely right for you, then there is no need for further concern. But there are a large number of people who feel stuck with celibacy either because their partner has abandoned sex; alternatively, they may not have a partner, or they want to shrink away from the tricky issues that carrying on with a sex life ignites.

LACK OF DESIRE

Lack of desire is a common sexual problem for couples that have been together for a while. Sometimes it affects just one partner; sometimes both feel a waning in their sexual attraction to each other. If you take a linear approach to sexual relationships – they start off hot, cool down over time and end up pretty frozen – then this is only to be expected. Sadly, this is probably the most common view of sex between couples in the West. It is also one of the reasons why so many couples split up. Novelty can be a powerful aphrodisiac and meeting someone new can re-awaken feelings that you may have thought you were no longer capable of.

A surprisingly high number of people think that finding a person who makes them feel like an excited teenager again is a good reason for ending their current relationship. There's nothing wrong with wanting to feel like an excited teenager – in fact there's a lot that's great about it. You become in touch with a sense of aliveness you may have otherwise lost, and it is thrilling to re-discover the delight your body can bring you. Where we go wrong, though, is in assuming that it is the

Wobbly
erections,
premature ejaculation,
lack of desire and worries
about ageing can be enough
to put you off sex
altogether

new person who is generating these good feelings in us – and that only he or she is capable of doing this. So we decide that the current partner must be ditched and the new one embraced. Now, on one level, it is true that the new person may be working a certain kind of magic. We may blossom in their attention and respond to the sexual signals they give out – but the key to living a more alive and connected life lies within us. It is not the gift of someone else. The Tantric approach to sexuality teaches us how to find this in ourselves.

Tantric philosophy is a reversal of the idea that a new relationship is always better and more exciting sexually. Tantrics believe that the longer you are with a partner, the more you know them, and the more closely connected you can become. Since Tantric sex is about intimacy and connection it is actually quite difficult to achieve this with someone you have only just met. According to the Taoists, it takes seven years to know your partner's body, seven years to know your partner's mind, and seven years to know your partner's spirit.

So where does all this leave you if you're in a partnership where you have become friends rather than lovers? What can you do to re-kindle desire between you? Accepting that the situation won't change without you changing your attitude to it is a helpful starting point. And if you also accept that you will have to put some energy into making that change, you are heading in the right direction. Couples who enjoy a flourishing sex life after years together are usually able to re-invent their relationship as time passes and their circumstances alter. They are also able to maintain separate but harmonious identities that energetically spark off each other.

Male and female levels of desire are both partly dependent on hormones, which fluctuate in the body. Work, family stresses and illness are also part of the tapestry that makes up our sexuality. Hormonally, the more sex your body has, the more it wants. The reverse is also true – the longer we go without fulfilling sexual contact the more likely we are to lose touch with our sexual self.

Boredom sets in when couples continue to make love in exactly the same way, at the same time and usually in the same place. Tantrics would say that it also occurs when you make love only with your genitals and your hearts and minds remain unconnected. Sex therapists usually recommend making love at different times of the day or trying out new sexual positions. While this can help, it doesn't address the main problem, which is the lack of intimacy and closeness that can separate a couple when they stop communicating about themselves.

INTIMACY

There is a school of thought which says that sex begins between a couple a day or two before they actually make love, and that when they begin to touch each other sexually they are bringing the positive and negative energy, as well as the stresses and joys, of the previous 48 hours with them.

Clearly, in an ideal world, you would have spent the time before making love with your partner relaxed and happy, either in your own space or else sharing time together – strolling through the countryside, perhaps, seeing a great movie or enjoying fun times with your children. The reality, however, might be a little different. Suppose you've been held up in a traffic queue for hours, had a row at work or been caring for a sick toddler?

To be successfully intimate with someone you need to be able to open your heart to them. Opening a heart which is chock-full of resentment, anger and frustration is unlikely to lead to a fulfilling sexual experience. Yes, there are people who claim to have great sex when they are angry. This is because the physical signals generated by the body – flushed cheeks, rapid breathing and a surge of energy – are not dissimilar to the signals we give off when we are sexually aroused. Making love to your partner to let off steam, however, may be one way of calming yourself down, but it is unlikely to leave them feeling good, and dumping your bad feelings on someone else is the very opposite of what Tantra is about.

The state you are in before you make love to your partner is important. Which is why Tantra workshops usually devote a hefty chunk of time to getting people to look at the agendas they take with them into sexual situations.

Although Tantra offers a powerfully different approach to sexual relationships, which can infuse them with a new energy and sense of aliveness, it won't be a 'quick-fix' for a relationship that makes you miserable and depressed. If your partnership is basically sound, Tantra has a lot to offer. But in adopting Tantric techniques, you are in effect shining a spotlight on both yourself and your partner, and your feelings about each other. If these are primarily good, but covered in a layer of dust and cobwebs, Tantra is the perfect tool to clean them up. But if you are in a relationship that is no longer right for you (or perhaps never was), doing a few Tantric exercises will not cover up the cracks.

COLIN, 51, MANAGEMENT TRAINER

'I was first introduced to Tantra on a week-long Tantra holiday in Turkey with my wife. We just assumed that she would get more out of it than me, but she didn't have anything like the incredible experiences that I had that week. I just went for a break with some friends and with an open mind; I didn't really have any expectations at all. But two of the exercises linked to energy that we did while we were there had a profoundly beneficial effect on me. So much so that by the end of the week I felt like a different person. Yet as a couple we had masses of issues between us and although we had more understanding of them afterwards, it didn't feel like we had been brought closer; in fact, we felt further apart. If there are cracks in your relationship, doing Tantra can make them feel like they get wider to begin with. I would like to carry on with Tantra, but you have to be prepared to cope emotionally and psychologically with the issues you need to look at as a result.'

One exercise used on Tantric workshops encourages people to learn to listen to each other without interrupting or offering their own interpretation of what they hear. They are not expected to give counter-arguments; they are simply required to listen. If this sounds ridiculously easy, try it with your partner or, if you are single, with a friend. You will be surprised at the strength of your desire to be heard and at how much you need to air your own opinions.

If you are planning a Tantric evening with your partner, make sure that you've both had some time to talk beforehand. This shouldn't be about mundane, everyday stuff to do with domestic arrangements; it should be the kind of conversation you had when you first met. And don't be tempted to think that you know everything there is to know about your partner by now, so there's no point. People change.

People change. Their ideas and opinions shift. They grow. Put an hour aside to update yourselves on each other. Take it in turns. One of you starts by talking for about half an hour about your thoughts and feelings and what you want out of life. As if you were explaining it to a stranger

Their ideas and opinions shift. They grow. Put an hour aside to update yourselves on each other. Take it in turns. One of you starts by talking for about half an hour about your thoughts and feelings and what you want out of life. As if you were explaining it to a stranger.

When in the listening role, just concentrate on paying attention. Don't let your mind wander onto your own stuff. Remember, listening isn't just a question of not interrupting. Genuinely take on board what your partner is saying. Then you can have your turn. If this sounds too 'stage-managed' for your tastes, ask yourself, 'Can I honestly say that I am in touch with my partner's thoughts on their life at the moment?' If the answer is yes (and you have checked that your assumption is right with your partner), then you don't need to do the exercise. But if you aren't 100 per cent sure, try it and see what comes up.

Of course, many couples lead distant, non-communicative lives under the same roof because they don't want to rock the boat or raise any issues they might feel uncomfortable handling. If this works for you and you are both happy with this state of affairs, then fair enough. But you may find you have trouble with Tantra.

ALTHOUGH

THERE'S A LOT OF TALK IN TANTRA

ABOUT CONNECTING YOUR HEART AND MIND

WITH YOUR PARTNER,

THIS IS NOT TO

SUGGEST THAT AS

INDIVIDUALS WE ARE

IN SOME WAY

LACKING AND

THEREFORE MADE

WHOLE BY THE

PRESENCE OF

ANOTHER PERSON.

CONNECTEDNESS IS

NOT THE SAME AS

CO-DEPENDENCY,

OR BEING IN A

SITUATION WHERE

YOU RELY ON GETTING YOUR GOOD FEELINGS

FROM SOMEONE ELSE

This is because Tantra is about connection, and if you are consciously choosing not to connect with your partner on some levels, then it is unlikely your heart will be sufficiently open to gain much benefit from Tantric practices.

Having sounded this warning, it may still be worth trying Tantra anyway if you are both keen to do so. Some couples have found that attempting Tantric techniques have made them re-assess the way they communicate in other areas of their lives. Or they have discovered that Tantra has awoken feelings and emotions they had lost sight of, and this revelation has prompted them to work harder on their relationship in other areas. If you know your relationship is not in a good state, keep your expectations of Tantra realistic. It is not a magic cure.

Although there's a lot of talk in Tantra about connecting your heart and mind with your partner (and the Divine, if you accept the spiritual aspect), this is not to suggest that as individuals we are in some way lacking and therefore made whole by the presence of another person. Connectedness is not the same as co-dependency, or being in a situation where you rely on getting your good feelings from someone else.

The most successful relationships flourish when two independent, fulfilled people choose to form a partnership where they may have different, but equal, roles. The words of Kahil Gibran in *The Prophet* are often quoted at wedding celebrations and they sum up a key truth about healthy relationships: '… you shall be together even in the silent memory of God. But let there be spaces in your togetherness. And let the winds of the heavens dance between you.'

Your relationship with your partner and your sexual relationship with them are practically one and the same thing. If you are not open with them outside bed, it is unlikely that you will be able to open up to them sexually. By the same token, when your sexual relationship is blooming, you will probably find that you are getting on together well in other respects too. (Relationship counsellors never cease to be amazed by the number of clients who are taken by surprise when re-establishing a good sex life leads to better friendship in other ways.)

So before you seek Tantra as a solution to sexual difficulties, be prepared to ask yourself the following questions:

1 Do I respect this person as a good friend?
2 Is my life better with this person than without them?
3 Do I want to grow with my partner and do I trust them to be there for me?

If you are uncertain about any or all of the above, it may be time to think carefully about your relationship before starting out on your Tantric path together. As I've said before — but it's worth repeating — Tantra can help heal wounds in individuals and relationships, but it's not a quick-fix solution if there is a major chasm between you.

To begin to reawaken desire you will need to spend time rebuilding an intimate connection with your partner. The talking exercise outlined above is a good place to start, as long as you remember, when doing it, to talk to your partner as if he or she were a stranger — that way you don't make assumptions on their behalf. The listening part is also key. Neither of you can build intimacy if you don't feel heard.

You will also need to make sure you spend quality time together — it doesn't necessarily have to be a weekend away, but it must be time that won't get abandoned in favour of your children, work, friends, a trip to the pub or your favourite hobby. At first, this need only be an hour or two a week. But once you have set the time aside, it should be sacrosanct. And you should stick to it — whether you are just going to talk or whether you are going to practise some Tantric techniques — even if you don't feel like it.

If you don't choose to become sexual, it is still important to continue touching each other. This way you exchange energy and release oxytocin (the cuddle hormone), which will increase your affection for your partner, and help you bond together. Creating a special space for this (see page 165) — even if it is just lighting some candles, dimming the lights and putting on some soft, heart-stirring music — will help too.

Don't feel you have to try every exercise in this book immediately. Changing the balance of a relationship to build greater intimacy and sexual connection takes a delicate touch. You can discuss with your partner beforehand how you might like to spend the hour or two you have dedicated to each other, or be completely spontaneous — see what works best for you. The main thing is not to give up. If you can, keep your excitement high but reduce your expectations of immediate results. Renewing a relationship brings rewards in all sorts of ways, but it takes time and effort. And there is no technique in the world that will transform your sex life forever if you don't have love in your heart.

PREMATURE EJACULATION

Problems with ejaculating too early are often linked with young men whose excitement reaches uncontrollable levels and leads them to ejaculate before their partner has got into their stride, sexually speaking. Tantric and Taoist practices are the ideal antidote to this as they teach men to draw their sexual energy away from their genitals and move it into other areas of their body, thus reducing the pressing desire to ejaculate.

Before discussing Tantric techniques, there's one practical thing you can do to help yourself if you suffer from premature ejaculation. Cut down on alcohol. Although millions of young men have discovered that alcohol inhibits their ability to ejaculate, drinking to slow you down is not a good idea. In effect, the alcohol acts as a kind of anaesthetic on your senses. In the same way that some men (apparently) recite the names of their favourite football team in an attempt to delay ejaculation, drinking alcohol is another ploy that leaves you less in touch with your body and your partner, and thus reduces your ability to notice and to control your sexual energy.

Whether you want to practise the Taoist principle of non-ejaculation, or take a more Tantric approach, which tends to be that you control your need to ejaculate until it suits you and your partner, there are several simple steps you can follow.

1   Stopping movement. This sounds like common sense, and it is. When you feel that your arousal rate is leading you to ejaculation, simply stop for a few strokes (or thrusts), for between 10 and 20 seconds, and allow the urge to ejaculate to wane.

2   Breathing. The breath is everything in Tantra. Deep breathing is vital in controlling your rate of arousal. Again, when you feel you are close to

ejaculating, take a deep breath and hold your breath for several moments until the urge starts to disappear.

3   Contracting the PC muscle. As you may have read in Chapter Two, the PC muscle surrounds the prostate, the gland that semen passes through during the ejaculation phase of orgasm. If you can learn to squeeze it when it begins to contract involuntarily, you can avoid reaching the 'point of no return' and ejaculating. Some men find this relatively easy; others find it tricky. But it's worth trying it a few times to see if you can get the hang of it.

4   Squeezing the penis. There are plenty of sex therapists that recommend this method of combating premature ejaculation. You place the first two fingers of either hand on the underside of your penis, place your thumb on the top and squeeze. The disadvantage of this is that if you are making love with your partner, you have to withdraw. Taoists take this one step further and suggest that in order to avoid having to withdraw, you practise squeezing your penis only 'with your mind'. It's understandable if this suggestion produces a quizzical raise of your eyebrows, although, as ever, you may be surprised at what works for you if you are willing to give it a try.

5   Pressing the perineum. Find what the Taoists call the Million Dollar Point between the base of your penis and your anus (see page 58). This exercise isn't for the faint-hearted – you need to push with your finger up to the first joint. You may find that it will decrease your erection slightly, but it will also prevent you ejaculating. The bonus with this approach is that you don't have to withdraw if you are making love – but you do need to know where to find it in the dark!

6   Scrotal tugging. This sounds wincingly painful, but it isn't if you do it properly. Because the testicles have to pull up close to the body for the semen to move out of the testes, pulling them away from your body can delay ejaculation. This is probably best practised for the first time during self-pleasuring. You simply circle the top of your scrotum with your thumb and forefinger and pull down firmly. (It can be more pleasant if your partner does this for you. She needs to get a firm grasp and then pull harder than she might think.)

7   Moving the sexual energy away from the genitals. As far as Tantrics and Taoists are concerned, this is the Number One route to delaying or cancelling ejaculation altogether, whichever is your choice. As you feel the energy start to build up in your pelvis, you imagine it travelling up your spine to your brain. Touch your palate with your tongue and then picture the energy moving down the front of your body and settling comfortably in your navel.

OTHER ERECTION DIFFICULTIES

Many of the sexual problems encountered by Western couples stem from the fairly narrow approach that most of us take towards sex – namely that a sexual encounter involves a man penetrating a woman with an erect penis until he reaches orgasm and ejaculates inside her. In this scenario, ideally, she reaches orgasm at the same time. End of story.

But for this story to have a happy ending, the man must get and maintain a reliable erection; he must manage not to ejaculate before his partner is sufficiently stimulated to reach orgasm herself and both parties have to time their orgasms (usually one orgasm for the man, and a couple for the woman if she's lucky) so they climax together. Often, the burden of expectation is on the man to manage this encounter, and if for some reason it does not go well – he loses his erection; he ejaculates prematurely or he does not 'give' his partner an orgasm – there is general disappointment all round.

This is clearly an over-generalisation, but it is not too far removed from reality. So, in the context of solving sexual problems linked to this template, where does Tantra fit in?

To begin with, Tantra takes away the goal of a couple working towards a man's single ejaculation and orgasm. It teaches men and women how to spread sexual energy throughout the whole body, so that it is no longer confined to the genitals. This means that as far as men are concerned, the pressure is off. Tantrics have a technique that enables a man to make love with a 'soft-on', described later in this chapter, so that it is not even necessary for him to have an erection.

If there is no
medical reason why
you should have
erection difficulties,
take a deep breath,
relax, and consider
trying a Tantric
approach to your
lovemaking

ROGER, 53, DOCTOR

'Most men's sexuality happens in their heads. While they are having a sexual experience, they are kind of watching themselves and comparing it to their fantasies, and all the advertising and movies, and perhaps giving themselves brownie points, thinking "This is what a real man does". It can mean that you end up not really relating to the woman that you are with; you may not even feel that much about her.

What I've discovered about Tantra is that it teaches you about sensory experience, so that you stay in your body. That way you restore sensitivity to the genitals and then you connect the genitals with your whole body by expanding the energy upwards. It is an entirely different, and in my experience, a much more satisfactory way of making love.'

According to one survey, more than 5 per cent of the UK male population is permanently impotent. A further 5 per cent have trouble with their erection about once a year. Roughly 15 per cent suffer quarterly and more than five million British men have experienced 'occasional erectile disorder'.

There are also physical and emotional causes that can make it difficult for a man to gain an erection, and if this is a persistent problem that is worrying you or your partner then it's always advisable to get it checked out with your doctor. If there is no medical reason why you should have erection difficulties, however, take a deep breath, relax, and consider trying a Tantric approach to your lovemaking. If the goal of an ejaculatory orgasm were to be taken away, how would you feel? It might be tempting to reply 'severely disappointed'. But we are not talking solely about loss here. We are talking about adopting an approach to sex that is likely to bring you a great deal more pleasure than you enjoyed before.

To begin with, you are endowed with several parts of your body – other than your penis – which can bring immense delight to a woman. In fact, few women reach orgasm through penetration alone. You have fingers to stroke your partner's skin and sexual organs, a tongue to lick with, and lips that you can use to caress, nibble and suck. (These are just the basics. There are inventive guys who can thrill a woman with their toes, elbows – great for certain types of massage – and their chest hair, and that's just for starters.) In fact, even if you have never had an erection problem in your life, it may be worth experimenting sometime with bringing as much pleasure as you can to your partner without using your penis. You could be more than pleasantly surprised at her response.

Equally, you may find it fun to play a less active role in your sexual relationship sometimes. Men can often get fed up with being the 'doers'. Which is why it may be an exciting change to reverse your normal sexual roles. You can take this as far as you like. For some couples it might mean 'dominant' and 'submissive' role-playing, complete with slave and master/mistress costumes; for others it could be a minor revolution such as the woman making love on top of her partner.

In acknowledging the influence of the Hindu gods, Shiva, the male, and Shakti, his female consort, Tantrics also accept that as individuals we are made up of male and female, or, as the Chinese think of it, yin and yang. This balance needs to exist both inside and outside us, and to be fully human we need to express both sides of ourselves.

In our Western, male-led perception of sexual relationships, we have lost sight of the fact that sometimes men want to nurture and women want to be bold and dominant. This doesn't have to be carried to extremes (unless you want to), but it will add another dimension to your relationship if you are both able to freely express other aspects of yourself.

Here are some useful techniques for solving erection difficulties.

MAKING LOVE WITH A 'SOFT-ON'

It is one of the great myths of sex, perpetrated mainly by the porn industry, that it is impossible to make love to a woman if you don't have an erection. Some women find the sensation of a man's penis becoming hard after it is inside them extremely arousing. Others just enjoy the closeness of a soft penis inside them, especially when their partner is giving energy and love from his heart at the same time. The following exercise can be done with the aim of gaining an erection inside the vagina, or it can be used simply to be close to your partner.

1   Make sure your partner is fully lubricated – ideally use a water-based lubricant inside her and on your penis.

2   Get on top – this is generally easier because the gravity helps move the blood into your penis (that's if you want an erection) and you are free to move as you wish. (The scissors positions is a good alternative to this – you replicate the shape of an open pair of scissors with your bodies; the woman lies on the left with the man's right leg between hers, while his left leg lies underneath her.)

3   Circle your thumb and forefinger around the base of your penis to form a ring and gently squeeze.

4   Carefully slide your penis inside your partner and begin gently thrusting, keeping your finger ring around the base of your penis.

5   Squeeze your buttocks and PC muscle to push blood into your genitals and focus on the sexual energy that is stirring inside your penis.

6   If your partner is happy to help, ask her to stimulate you by playing with your testicles, perineum (see page 57) or anus (only if you find this pleasurable, of course).

7   Adjust the tightness of your finger according to how firm you want your erection to be.

According to Tantra teacher Leora, a man may also find it highly pleasurable to leave his penis inside the vagina, simply to rest there, without any intention of gaining an erection. 'It is a completely different approach,' she explains. 'You have minimal movement. At first it just feels like you're not doing anything, but if you both relax and wait for the feelings to take over it can be incredibly beautiful.'

This 'soft-style' lovemaking is also easier when you are lying side-by-side in the 'spoons' position, where you both lie with your knees bent, with the man behind the woman. You can also trying breathing through each of the chakras together in this position (see page 21), simply by placing your hands on the woman's base chakra and breathing love and energy into each centre, moving up to the crown and then down again.

Making love while you are both fully clothed

It is also perfectly possible to 'make love' to someone when you are both fully clothed. Tantric sexuality is about exchanging energy with your partner, or moving your own sexual energy around your body to bring you to into a blissful state. As a couple, you may not want penetrative sex all the time, but you may still want to be close and intimate with each other. The following exercise allows you to make love with your partner without any physical sexual contact:

Sit facing your partner; place your left hand on his or her heart centre and cover his or her left hand with your right hand. Look into each other's left eye and breathe together. Imagine receiving love and energy from your partner as you inhale, and giving out love and energy to your partner as you exhale.

Have you ever started to make love with someone and felt that you were entirely disconnected emotionally and mentally? Well, this simple process allows you to harmonise your energies and build a surprisingly deep level of connection with another person. At the same time, it will help you feel more balanced too.

Growing older

In the same way that in the West we tend to regard sexual relationships as linear – starting off exciting and dwindling into dullness – we think of great sex happening when we are young and the excitement fading as we get older. In fact, when you are 20 it is hard to imagine anyone over 50 ever making love.

As you grow older you realise how ridiculous this assumption is. But if you were simply to look at the media images in our society you could be forgiven for thinking that sex happens only between the ages of 17 and 30 (for women), perhaps 40 for men. But according to one US survey of more than 4000 men and women, 80 per cent of married men and women over 70 remain sexually active and 58 per cent have sex at least once a week.

Quite apart from the fact that it has been scientifically proven that an active sex life helps you keep fitter and younger looking – one of the benefits of sex hormones and endorphins rushing around the body – men and women become sexually more compatible as they grow older. Hormonally-speaking, testosterone regulates sexual interest in both men and women. While a woman's body produces lower amounts of oestrogen after the menopause, it continues to produce the same small amount of testosterone that it always has. Many women discover that after the menopause their interest in sex unexpectedly increases. Apart from no longer worrying about an unwanted pregnancy, they may find that their family or work responsibilities diminish and they have more time to themselves and to spend with their partners.

After peaking in his twenties, a man experiences a reduction in the amount of testosterone in his body as he grows older, which means that his sexual responses tend to slow down. A man over 50 will need significantly more genital stimulation to get and to maintain an erection. The erection itself may also be less firm and upright. This doesn't normally affect his levels of desire, though, and as a result sex can become a more harmonious and better-matched experience for both of you.

A medical note: certain prescription drugs can have a profound effect on reducing your libido. It is estimated that around a quarter of all cases of impotence are caused by prescription drugs that men take to combat heart disease, high blood pressure, depression and other medical conditions. Some desire-dampening ingredients are also found in over-the-counter medication for symptoms of colds or 'flu. These same drugs can also affect women's levels of sexual desire and ability to orgasm. If you are prescribed drugs by your doctor it is worth asking if they have any side-effects that might affect your sexual response.

Healing positions

No book about Tantra would be complete without some description of positions for lovemaking. (I have to mention my favourite Tantric joke here. The 79-year-old British playwright and novelist John Mortimer was once asked about Tantric sex. He replied: 'It's very slow. My favourite position is called The Plumber. You stay in all day but nobody comes.')

Seriously, if you are simply looking for variety, try reading the Kama Sutra, which outlines 64 sexual positions ranging from the familiar to the acrobatic. Just their names are a treat. Embrace of the Rice and Sesame Seed (the partners lie very close together and the man places his leg between the woman's thighs) and Embrace of a Twining Creeper (standing up with the woman's legs around the back of the man's thighs) are two of the more poetic-sounding ones.

The basic variations examined here are straightforward: woman on top; man on top; man from behind; side by side and sitting opposite each other.

Woman on top

This is the easiest position for a man who wants to control his ejaculation and become multi-orgasmic. It is simpler to relax like this and to concentrate on moving energy up your spine. From a woman's perspective, keep the glans of the penis in the most sensitive outer 5 cm (2 in) of the vagina (virtually any man will instinctively want to plunge in much deeper when he is on top) and you can direct the penis to your G-spot. Equally, male or female fingers can stimulate the clitoris at the same time.

This is a good position to use in the later stages of pregnancy and for men who are older, or not in the best of health, as it requires much less energy than anything else.

Man on top

This position sometimes gets a bad press as being deemed too traditional. It is often referred to as 'the missionary position,' after it was advocated by white missionaries who travelled abroad, trying to convert non-Christians in Victorian times. These were the years when women were supposed to regard sex only as a patriotic duty, and were instructed to 'lie back and think of England'.

This is to deny the enjoyment that many people get from this position. It allows you and your partner to look into each other's eyes, and to kiss while you make love. The woman can run her hand up her partner's spine to help him draw his energy upwards and if a man rests on his hands or elbows, he is able to control his thrusting or screwing techniques to satisfy his partner. The only major disadvantage

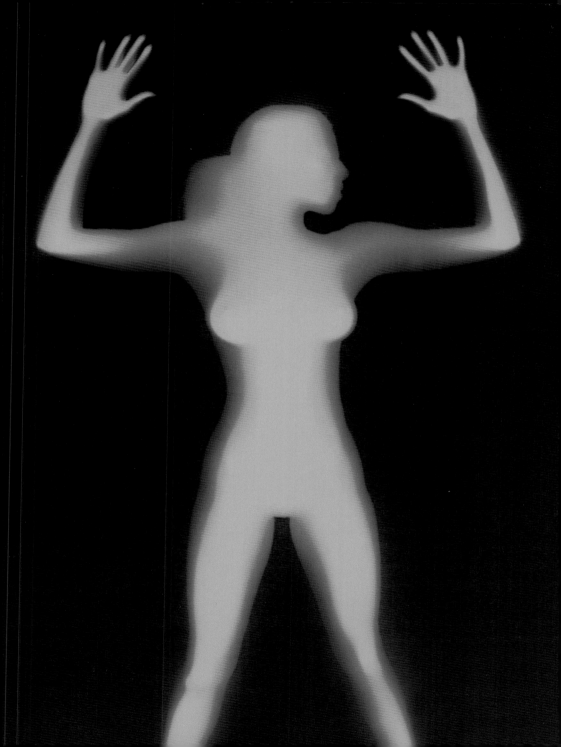

of this position is that in a lot of cases the penis misses the G-spot unless a man tilts his hips and changes the angle of his erection. Alternatively, a pillow (ideally crescent-shaped) under the woman's buttocks can remedy this and allows deeper penetration (as does resting the woman's legs on her partner's shoulders).

MAN FROM BEHIND

Known rather inelegantly as the Congress of the Cow in the Kama Sutra, this position can be highly arousing for both sexes. While you may be denied eye contact, this position is one of the best for helping women to achieve multiple orgasms, especially when the woman's body is angled downwards or lying flat, when it is relatively easy to reach the G-spot with the penis. In this position, too, the vagina is usually especially tight and if a woman squeezes her thighs together, this increases, as well as making it easier for her to contract her PC muscle.

SIDE BY SIDE

A relaxing way to make love, although it may be tricky to maintain as penetration is rather shallow. The Taoists recommend as a pleasant slow-down after more energetic sex. If you are face to face it helps bring you both back to a sense of balance and harmony.

SITTING OPPOSITE EACH OTHER

This is the ultimate Tantric sex position. Known by the Tantrics as Yab-Yom (mother–father), this is when a man sits in a cross-legged position and the woman sits astride him with her legs partially around his back. This allows maximum spiritual and emotional connection and it is the easiest position in which to circulate energy between you. To actively make love like this, you both need to rock your pelvises, or at the very least exercise both sets of PC muscles.

This position is usually only adopted after at least an hour of foreplay and penetration when the energy chakras have been awakened and energy is moving upwards in both partners. At this point the lovers enter a kind of meditation. Holding each other very close and breathing in synchronicity, the penis remains hard inside while the vagina relaxes and contracts with the in and out breath. The couple circulate energy between their bodies and build a feeling of expansion between themselves and the universe. At this point some people see coloured lights, others have a sense of moving outside their bodies and being aware of a connectedness with something much greater than themselves. They may each experience a full-body orgasm where energy rushes up from the base of the spine to the crown of the head, leaving little (or large) tremors in its wake.

Either way, this form of union has a profound effect on people who practise it. Not only do they frequently feel united spiritually with the rest of the world, they feel especially linked through a powerful bond of love to their partner. It's probably the furthest thing on earth from a quick shag on a Friday night when you are both feeling exhausted.

Having said this, taking up Tantra is not about setting goals for yourself and getting disappointed if you don't achieve them rapidly. It is more about choice. If you have knowledge you are able to make a choice about the way you explore your sexuality and the way that you relate to yourself and your partner. Understanding Tantra gives you that choice.

ABUSIVE RELATIONSHIPS

Tantra celebrates our joy in sex, but for some people sex has never been a joyful business. In fact, it may be the very opposite. Sexual abuse is a broad term that we tend to connect with children who have been mentally and physically overpowered by adults. For some people, this legacy lasts well into their adult lives, infecting their relationships with others at many levels. For others, it is their adult relationships that have wrecked their ability to have happy sex lives. Either way, there are plenty of people who have been wounded by others sexually, and Tantra offers a path of emotional healing.

Think extremely carefully before you try Tantra with your partner if you feel you are in a damaging relationship. Tough as this may sound, if you can't trust your partner to respect you, or you feel that you can't respect them, Tantric practices simply won't work.

Having said this, there are thousands of people who have experienced physical or sexual abuse in the past who have moved on from those harmful relationships and found Tantra a path of healing. My suggestion is that if you are in a partnership with someone who is abusive towards you in any way, and you are unable to change that pattern, seek immediate help to get out of it. Then, when you have walked away from the abuse, you may find that Tantra is an enormous help in regaining your personal and sexual confidence.

Rachel, 34, lecturer

'I had never had sex and then I was raped when I was sixteen. It was horrific. For about two years after that I just didn't want to have sex with anyone, and when I did I felt a lot of anger. My feelings about sex got distorted, for me it was a way of expressing anger rather than love. Over the years, I seemed to get more and more closed up. Then I would find myself being with a man and doing stuff that I really didn't want to do because I wanted to please him. I heard about Tantra and I decided to go on a series of workshops and it changed my life. I experienced a lot of respect and tenderness from men in the workshop environment which was the complete opposite of my first experience. I learnt that sexuality and intimacy is so much more than bonking. And I don't feel as obsessed by sex as I used to be. I've got more respect for myself and I know what my boundaries are.

Because of what happened to me as a teenager, for a long time I blamed myself and I wouldn't approach men or allow myself to be sexy or flirtatious. Now I can do that much more and I feel I can celebrate just being in my body. Sex has become a whole body experience for me. Even in the 21st century, there is a lot of fear and ignorance about sex. There are still so many young people fumbling around, not knowing quite what to do. So many people are really missing out on a big part of life. Tantra has shown me a whole world that I didn't know existed.'

Tantric workshops are not for everyone, but for people who have experienced bad relationships they can be a turning point. Equally, a genital massage from a loving partner can also be an important step on the path to sexual healing.

Tantrics believe that memories of our physical experiences are stored in the cells of our bodies. This isn't a theory that you will find taught at medical school, but it may be that science will catch up with this idea one day. Tantrics work on the principle that gentle massage can release trauma or buried pain, and that this kind of massage can re-sensitise areas that may have become deadened or cut off from the rest of the body.

How to give a woman a sexual healing massage

This isn't something you can do playfully. If you want to help your partner in this way, make sure that she feels completely safe. Prepare your room carefully, check that it is warm and inviting and ensure that your every movement and touch is gentle and loving. It is good to begin this massage by building up her energy through dancing or Kundalini shaking (see page 149). During the course of the massage, encourage your partner to breathe deeply and match her breathing yourself. If, by any chance, she becomes upset, gently ask her if she wants you to carry on or stay exactly as you are, or to stop and just hold her.

In some types of massage it can be helpful to limit the amount you talk so the giver and the receiver can concentrate on their physical sensations. But in a sexual healing massage, communication is very important. The person receiving the massage needs to share what she does and doesn't like and she needs to be able to talk about any feelings that come up for her. If you are the giver, all you have to do when she starts to talk is to listen. Nothing else. It may be that she doesn't want to talk during the massage. If that is the case, be prepared to listen afterwards, but don't interrogate her. Now is not the time to seek an ego boost by asking 'Was I OK?'

1   Your partner should lie on her back, comfortably supported by pillows or cushions. You can sit by her side or between her open legs, which should also be supported by pillows or cushions. Look into her eyes and start to harmonize your breath (take the lead from her and match your breath accordingly). Place

your left hand on her heart centre and your right hand over her pelvis. (If you are left-handed you may want to do this the other way around.)

2   After several minutes of concentrating on your breathing, begin to massage her entire body. Brush energy away from the pelvic area, upwards towards the abdomen and down her arms and well as along her thighs and legs.

3   Now you can move on to the area around her pelvis, her groin and the tops of her thighs. A surprising amount of tension can be stored here. Check whether the pressure you are using is too light, too firm or just right.

4   Just before you approach the genital area, cup your hand over the pubic area and place the other on her heart and gently look into her eyes.

5   After gently stroking the outside of this area, rub a small amount of water-based lubricant on to your fingers (warm it first) and begin slowly massaging the outside of her genitals. Don't rush. If you want to, talk to your partner – if you think she's beautiful, let her know. Just to warn you – this can be an unnerving experience for some women. Most women are not used to men gazing like this. For some women, it can feel more intimate than having sex, so don't worry if she tenses up a bit. Just reassure her that you are going to take care of her and carry on, if she is OK about it.

6   Gently squeeze the outer lips of the vulva between your thumb and forefinger and slide up and down the length of each lip. Do the same to the inner lips. (Check out page 41 if you aren't exactly sure of female geography.)

7   All the while, make sure that your partner is enjoying the pace and pressure you are applying. If she is feeling pretty relaxed, it's time to move on to the clitoris. Stroke it with small circles. Support your partner to relax into any erotic feelings. You can move the energy outwards by stroking it away from the pelvis again, or your can build it up by stroking and circling a nipple with your free hand.

8   At your partner's invitation you can slowly slide the middle finger of your right hand (or left if you are left-handed) into her vagina. Slowly explore the inside in every direction and massage it. You can do this in small circles, you can make tiny up-and-down movements or you can just hold her from the inside,

especially if she becomes upset. If she does become distressed, it's better to stay inside and very still, rather than withdrawing, unless, of course, she asks you to.

9 With your palm facing upwards, move your middle finger in a 'Come here' motion. This will probably put you in contact with her G-spot, which is a spongy area of tissue under the pubic bone (see Chapter Two). If this feels uncomfortable for your partner, stop moving for a while. When she feels better, you can move your finger side to side, back and forth or in circles. You can also slowly vary the pressure and speed.

10 Keep massaging until she tells you to stop. Maintain eye contact. Withdraw your hand very, very gently and respectfully. Hold her and cuddle while she relaxes afterwards. Don't be alarmed if she gets upset. It is not you that is causing her distress. By giving her a gentle sexual healing massage you are helping to heal her and open her up to a heightened capacity to experience orgasm, in the same way that an osteopath can release a stiff neck. It may take time but it will pay dividends later. A sexual healing massage is one of the most special things a partner can give.

How to give a man a sexual healing massage

Although it is women who tend to corner the popular imagination in terms of receiving physical, mental or sexual abuse from men, there are many men who can testify that it works the other way around too. However, it is much tougher for men to talk about. A bloke complaining to his mates in the pub that his partner mistreats him is not likely to get the sympathetic hearing that a woman in the same situation might expect. But like women, men can be hurt sexually, as well as physically or emotionally.

There is a small, but growing movement (more vocal in the United States than in Britain) that believes men who are circumcised as babies experience a form of mutilation that can adversely affect them in later life. It can also be difficult for a man to see his penis as an integral part of himself, instead of viewing it as a kind of external rod that has little to do with his heart. Which is why a massage from a loving partner, who is prepared to touch his penis in a healing, non-sexual way can be a transforming experience.

The aim of this massage is to allow a man to let go and relax into the sensations in his body without feeling that he has to do anything about them. It doesn't matter whether he has an erection or not at any stage of the massage. If he is lying on his back gravity is drawing blood away from his penis, so he is less likely to be erect. But an erection is not a reflection of how much he is enjoying the massage. A man may experience intense pleasure, whether or not he is erect. He may experience an orgasm, or he may not – that is not the point. It can be difficult for a man to be passive, but if he can give up the expectation that this exercise is something he is in control of, and accept that the only thing he has to do is to relax and sink into pleasure, then he is on the right track.

1   Cuddle your partner and place your hand over his heart centre, send love and energy into his heart through your breath. Match your breathing to his. Encourage him to breathe deeply and slowly if he is feeling tense.
2   Allow him to relax in your arms. Hold him close and in a way that feels comfortable for you both.
3   It can help raise the energy levels in your partner's pelvis if he lifts his buttocks off the floor and bounces them lightly up and down for a minute or two. Alternatively, you can massage his buttocks to get the energy flowing in this area.
4   Pelvic bouncing usually encourages the body to begin to shake. As he shakes, stroke your hands down his thighs and legs into his feet, resting your hands over his feet. This will make him feel grounded.
5   The next stage is to allow your partner to release his energy and relax into the sensations he has created. Place one hand 5 cm (2 in) below his navel and the other over his heart. Match your breathing and begin to breathe deeply.
6   Begin to massage the muscles around the pubic bone, down to the muscles that support the pelvic floor and the groin. Begin just above his pubic hair and massage down into the groin. If your partner is ticklish (and a lot of men are

not used to being touched in this area) use a firm touch. Continue to massage down into his thighs.

7   Gently massage behind his testicles. Check with your partner what kind of pressure he likes best. You can move on from here to the perineum, which is where the spongy tissue of the base of the penis goes deep into the pelvic floor.

8   Cradle a testicle in one hand. (This can make men nervous.) Ask your partner to relax and breathe deeply. It may take several minutes before he feels fully comfortable with this. Move on to the other testicle when he is ready.

9   The skin of the scrotum can be stroked – ask your partner for his preferences. You can also feel the tube that carries the seminal fluid from the testicles to the penis inside the scrotum; some men enjoy this being lightly stroked.

10 If you are the recipient, don't try to constrict any erotic energy that may arise, but don't be in sway to it either. Just breathe into it and stay with the experience of just receiving. If you are the giver and you can see that your partner is becoming aroused, you can stroke the energy away from his genitals by moving your hand upwards to his heart area. You can also move it across his chest down to his fingertips and down his thighs into his legs and feet.

11 Massage his penis from the scrotum up. It's easier to massage a penis that isn't aroused. If he becomes very aroused, disperse the energy away to the rest of his body by rubbing the penis up along the stomach.

12 Play with the idea of stimulating his penis and his Million Dollar Point (see page 58) at the same time.

13 If ejaculation does occur, it is usually intense and satisfying and the orgasmic feeling spreads throughout the body. But bear in mind that this is not a goal for either of you.

14 If you are the giver, don't expect anything in return. Don't feel 'It's my turn now'. Simply let your partner rest and relax afterwards.

9

SEX AND
SPIRIT

The writer Victor Hugo once said that 'to love another person is to see the face of God'. And it's true that especially in the early stages of being in love, we can feel a sense of ecstasy and wonder. Meeting someone we love can bring out the best in us. We become better people; more thoughtful, more giving and more inclined to see the other person's point of view.

But it is rare for us to stay in this state of harmony and unity. All too often, we sink back into our separateness. Within weeks or months we may feel let down or misunderstood by our loved one; we may feel taken for granted, or even as though we had fallen in love with the 'wrong' person.

This is because we lose track of what love is. It is not about making someone feel good because they make you feel good (although that's a small part of it). Romantic feelings, powerful and all-encompassing as they are at times, are just one tiny aspect of love, and to build a relationship purely on romance or physical attraction to another person is like trying to engineer a house on shifting sand.

Think, if you can, of a couple you know who have a truly loving and happy relationship. You may notice that their love does not extend only to each other. They are loving and supportive to friends and family in their wider circle too. This is because they are in touch with something bigger than romantic love. They are tuned in to 'universal love'. This means they have good feelings about themselves, their partner and the world around them. They have their own identities and sense of purpose and they share their partnership as two whole people who are together voluntarily. They are not bound by neediness, fear or insecurity.

Although Tantra can be a valuable tool for adding sparkle to your sex life, and it is absolutely fine if you use this book only for that purpose, that in itself is a fairly limited objective. The prime aim of Tantra is to put you more closely in touch with universal love. The practices outlined in this book, especially those connected with energy, were originally designed for this.

Tantra is not just about having a better time in bed; it is about waking up to the joys of the world around you, and understanding that your sexual energy is a fantastic vehicle for reaching a place of joy and contentment either by yourself or with a partner. It is about learning to infuse the rest of your life with this energy, so that you are more light-hearted and in touch with your thinking ability, your senses and your emotions. (If you have ever felt happier after good sex you already have an inkling of what I'm talking about.)

The process of engaging your sexual energy in this way can take time. But that doesn't matter. Every journey begins with a single step, and whether you are trying Tantra by yourself or with a partner, making an open-hearted effort to explore your sexuality will be rewarded, probably sooner rather than later.

Within a couple, Tantra is a shared journey. It is not about one person imposing on another. It involves building levels of passion and intimacy without power games or put-downs.

The word intimacy has its roots in a Latin word meaning 'innermost' and true intimacy is about being willing to open your heart to another person without fearing that they will reject you or find you lacking. As the structure of Tantra is about honouring and respect, reaching a greater level of intimacy with another person is automatically easier if you follow a Tantric approach. And in a world where the means of communication are everywhere but deep and honest communication is increasingly rare, Tantric practices are a route to regaining this kind of intimacy that is so often lost when people lead busy and pressured lives.

CATHY, 51, PUBLIC RELATIONS MANAGER

'Tantra has had a very calming effect on me. It has made me more tolerant of other people, including my husband. We have started to understand each other better. We've learned to give each other space and Tantra has rekindled our love as well as our friendship and closeness.'

ROGER, 47, COMPANY DIRECTOR

'Tantra has given me a sense of inner peace and the knowledge that our love is unbreakable. The depth of our love is enlightening and it gives us strength. And to practise Tantra you don't have to make an effort because you don't really feel like it. It is not like going to the gym. You do have to make time for it, but it isn't a drag because it is so worth the effort.'

If you are looking for more intimacy, connection and ecstasy in your sex life, it is worth remembering the key Tantric practices:

1 Be aware of your breathing, breathe deeply into your belly, especially when you are sending sexual energy around your body.

2 Gaze into each other's eyes.

3 Relax rather than tense into sexual excitement.

Some basic Taoist guidelines are also useful. The first is to remember that for relaxing and harmonizing with your partner, it is best to place similar body parts together. So lips press against lips, hands against hands and genitals against genitals. If you want to stimulate and excite each other, you should place dissimilar parts of your body together: lips to genitals, fingers to mouth and so on.

Another is that the person who moves most – usually the person on top – is the one who gives the most energy (positive or negative). It is therefore helpful for the person underneath to move as much as they are comfortable with in order to balance the movement of the person on top. In the West we tend to think that the person on top in a sexual union is the dominant, more powerful partner. The Taoists, however, believe that the person on top is serving the person underneath them by giving the most healing energy to them. Taoist practice is about using passion to heal your partner, and never as a weapon to take charge of them.

Although Tantra is a spiritual path, for many people who have begun to adopt a Tantric approach, it is the practical effects in their lives that make the greatest impact at first.

CATHERINE, 33, OCCUPATIONAL THERAPIST

'After my first Tantric workshop I felt that there had been some sort of shift inside me. It was like a release and I knew I was different within myself; I was in a much more peaceful, stiller place. I am an occupational therapist and I found that I could hold on to what people were saying and do it with much better empathy, I guess.

I also found I was treating people differently, in a more holistic way, and I felt much more creative. I started writing poetry. Obviously, after one workshop I'm not a Tantric expert, but the emphasis on taking time and honouring the other person and reconnecting with those basics has made me think that I will definitely bring a different awareness to my next relationship.'

'Learning about Tantra has brought me so many blissful experiences. The phrase that comes to my mind is that it is like a heaven on earth.'

IAN, 44, IT SPECIALIST

'For me Tantra is not a spiritual experience. My wife and I are using it to expand our focus and to open up blockages in our relationship and to gain intimacy with each other. We didn't get into it to be spiritual; personally, I'm uncomfortable with that aspect of it. For us it is the physical and emotional aspects of Tantra that work.

What has been hugely helpful for me has been the experience of going on Tantra courses, being close to other people when they are open and expressing things that are normally hidden. I wasn't comfortable with intimacy and being around women. Tantra has helped save my marriage.

I think it works in a way that is invisible. Sometimes I think, "What has this got to do with anything?" But I've been doing it for three years now and my wife says that I have changed so much, I'm a different person. We have been able to speak about things and gone through really difficult times that otherwise would have torn us apart. We have started to communicate on a much deeper level. Tantra has been the most beneficial force for change in my life in the past three years.'

Centuries ago, Tantric teaching was often passed on in poetic or verse form. I think this extract from 'The Invitation', by Oriah Mountain Dreamer, works well as a modern equivalent. Certainly it sums up much of what this book is about.

The Invitation

It doesn't interest me what you do for a living.

I want to know what you ache for, and if you dare to dream of meeting your heart's longing.

It doesn't interest me how old you are. I want to know if you will risk looking like a fool for love, for your dream, for the adventure of being alive.

It doesn't interest me what planets are squaring your moon. I want to know if you have touched the centre of your own sorrow, if you have been opened by life's betrayals or have become shrivelled and closed from fear of further pain. I want to know if you can sit with pain, mine or your own, without moving to hide it or fade it or fix it.

I want to know if you can be with joy, mine or your own, if you can dance with wildness and let the ecstasy fill you to the tips of your fingers and toes without cautioning us to be careful, to be realistic, to remember the limitations of being human …

I want to know if you can see beauty, even when it's not pretty, every day, and if you can source your own life from its presence …

It doesn't interest me who you know or how you came to be here. I want to know if you will stand in the centre of the fire with me and not shrink back.

It doesn't interest me where or what or with whom you have studied. I want to know what sustains you, from the inside, when all else falls away.

I want to know if you can be alone with yourself and if you truly like the company you keep in the empty moments.

As this poem suggests, Tantra is about entering fully into every aspect of your life and connecting wholeheartedly with the gifts of love and sex. And it is through this connection that you contact real joy, which spiritually aware people describe as the presence of the Divine, or God.

According to Tantra teacher John:

'Technically, Tantra is not so much about pepping up your sex life as seeing yourself and your partner with new eyes. It is like a wake-up call. You can come back to a kind of simple freshness, because ordinarily our senses become very jaded. It is about harnessing those energies of love and sex that are capable of coming into our lives and busting them apart. But instead of finding ourselves doing unsuitable, crazy things you are working with those energies consciously and for your own benefit.'

RACHEL, 34, LECTURER

'Learning about Tantra has brought me so many blissful experiences. It has helped me shake off depression and anger and opened up a whole new perspective on my life. The phrase that comes to my mind is that it is like a heaven on earth.'

Tantra is about openness, respect and acknowledging that there is more to life than grabbing instant gratification at the expense of others. In order to receive, you have to be prepared to give. Or to do as you would be done by. And this isn't a principle that only applies in the bedroom. Tantrics use their worldly experience of sex as a gateway to a wider perspective on our existence. And as a result they find that their whole lives – not just their sex lives – are infinitely richer and more rewarding.

TANTRA WORKSHOPS

If you are interested in finding out more about Tantra, I recommend attending a Tantra workshop. While no one spiritual path is necessarily better than another, there will be one that is the most appropriate for you, and the same applies to Tantra teachers. If you are looking for any kind of teacher, your best bet is to start with one who has a decent track record. Bear in mind the following questions:

1   How much teaching experience do they have?

2   When, where and with whom did they train, and for how long?

3   Can they give you references from two or three people who have studied with them?

4   What will be the proportion of teacher and helpers to course participants? (Around one to seven is a good ratio. More than that and you can't be sure that you will get the right help if you need it.)

5   Does the course leader, or any of his/her assistants, have any medical or psychological training? It isn't necessary for a qualified medical doctor to be present, but you want to be sure that there's someone around who knows about first aid if you have an accident, and that the teacher has some psychological understanding.

6   Listen to your gut instincts. Even if a friend is enthusiastic about their experience with a certain teacher, he/she may not be right for you, so don't be talked into learning about Tantra with someone about whom you have serious reservations.

7   Always meet the Tantra teacher first. Ideally, attend an introductory evening before embarking on a full weekend training. (A reputable teacher will be keen to meet you too. They will want to screen out people who may be unsuited to working with others on a Tantra course.)

For further details contact Leora Lightwoman at:

Diamond Light Tantra

P.O. Box 38204, London NW3 6YZ

Tel: 08700 780584

www.diamondlighttantra.com

email: info@diamondlighttantra.com

Leora Lightwoman's CD and video, *Tantric Sexuality*, are available from the address above.

FURTHER READING

Aldred, Caroline *Divine Sex*, Carroll & Brown Publishers Ltd (2000)

Anand, Margo *The Art of Sexual Ecstasy*, Penguin Putnam Inc. (1989)

Anderson, William *The Waking Dream*, Hutchinson Benham Ltd (1983)

Arewa, Caroline Shola *Way of Chakras*, Thorsons (2001)

Berman, Jennifer & Laura *For Women Only*, Virago Press (2001)

Bodansky, Steve & Vera *Extended Massive Orgasm*, Vermilion (2000)

Chia, Mantak and Maneewan *The Multi-Orgasmic Couple*,
    HarperCollins Publishers, Inc. (2000)

Chia, Mantak and Maneewan *Cultivating Female Sexual Energy*,
    Healing Tao Books (1986)

Chia, Mantak *The Multi-Orgasmic Man*, Thorsons (1996)

Cox, Tracey *Hot Sex*, Corgi Books (1998)

Craze, Richard *Tantric Sexuality*, Hodder & Stoughton (1999)

Ensler, Eve *The Vagina Monologues*, Virago Press (2001)

Hooper, Anne *Pocket Kama Sutra*, Dorling Kindersley Ltd (1996)

Joannides, Paul *Guide to Getting It On!*, Vermilion (2000)

Johnson, Anne *The Essential Book of Tantric Sex*, Michael O'Mara Books Ltd (2000)

Lacroix, Nitya *Tantric Sex*, Anness Publishing Ltd (1999)

Lee, Dr Victoria, *Soulful Sex*, Conari Press (USA) (1996)

Linn, Denise *Feng Shui for the Soul*, Ebury Press (1999)

Lorius, Cassandra *Tantric Sex*, Thorsons (1999)

Odier, Daniel *Tantric Quest*, Inner Traditions (1996)

Paget, Lou *The Big O*, Judy Piatkus (Publishers) Ltd (2001)

Pease, Allan & Barbara *Why Men Don't Listen & Women Can't Read Maps*,
    Orion Books Ltd (2001)

Ramsdale, David and Ellen *Sexual Energy Ecstasy*, Bantam Books (1993)

Sarita, Ma Ananda & Geho, Swami Anand *Tantric Love*, Gaia Books Ltd (2001)

Shaw, Miranda *Passionate Enlightenment*, Princeton University Press (1994)

Singh, Guru Dharam and O'Keeffe, Darryl *Kundalini: The Essence of Yoga*,
    Gaia Books Ltd (2002)

Smith, Gilly *Tantra & The Tao*, Robinson Publishing Ltd (1996)

Stubbs, Kenneth Ray *Tantric Massage*, Ebury Press (1991)

Walker, Barbara G. *The Woman's Encyclopaedia of Myths and Secrets*, HarperSanFrancisco

Wikoff, Johanina & Romaine, Deborah S *The Complete Idiot's Guide To The Kama
    Sutra*, Macmillan USA, Inc (2000)